MW00534392

Bridgewater Triangle

Christopher Balzano

Schiffer Publishing Ltd

4880 Lower Valley Road • Atglen, PA 19310

Ouija is a registered trademark
of Hasbro Inc.

Other Schiffer Books by Christopher Balzano

Dark Woods: Cults, Crime, & Paranormal in the Freetown State Forest, 978-0-7643-2799-5, $14.95

Other Schiffer Books on Related Subjects
Boston's Haunted History, 978-0-7643-2874-9, $12.95
Haunted Massachusetts, 978-0-7643-2662-2, $12.95
Provincetown Discovered, 0-88740-061-2, $12.95

Copyright © 2008 by Christopher Balzano
Library of Congress Control Number:
2008927193

All rights reserved. No part of this work may
be reproduced or used in any form or by any
means—graphic, electronic, or mechanical,
including photocopying or information storage
and retrieval systems—without written
permission from the publisher.

The scanning, uploading and
distribution of this book or any
part thereof via the Internet or via
any other means without
the permission of the
publisher is illegal
and punishable by law.
Please purchase only
authorized editions and
do not participate in or
encourage the electronic
piracy of copyrighted
materials.

"Schiffer," "Schiffer
Publishing Ltd. &
Design," and the
"Design of pen and
ink well" are registered
trademarks of Schiffer
Publishing Ltd.

Cover by
Bruce Waters

Designed by
Stephanie Daugherty
Type set in Humanist
521BT/NewBskvill BT

ISBN: 978-0-7643-3006-3

Printed in the
United States of America

For our complete selection of fine books
on this and related subjects, please visit our
website at www.schifferbooks.com. You may
also write for a free catalog.

Schiffer Publishing's titles are available at
special discounts for bulk purchases for sales
promotions or premiums. Special editions, including
personalized covers, corporate imprints, and excerpts,
can be created in large quantities for special needs. For
more information, contact the publisher.

We are always looking for people to write books on new
and related subjects. If you have an idea for a book, please
contact us at proposals@schifferbooks.com.

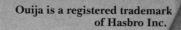

Dedication

To my wife, Jill who, through the hours and the missed sleep, kept me expecting something better.

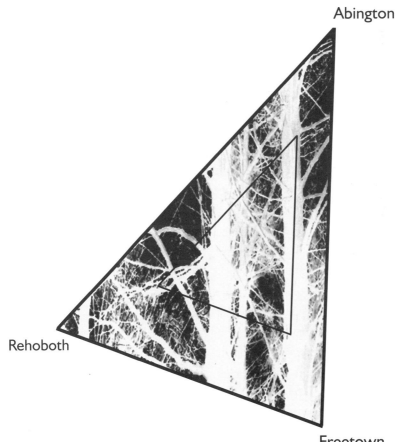

Acknowledgments

There are two legs that make this book stand. They are the researchers who most instructed and inspired me and without them people would only still be whispering about the Triangle. Loren Coleman and Chris Pittman deserve all the credit for this book, and I thank them for getting the word out there. This book would not have been possible without the help of the Spooky Crew at "Spooky Southcoast"; Tim Weisberg, Matt Costa, and Matt Moniz, who also was my co-investigator on several of these cases. They enabled me to talk to people in the area and sent stories my way. Thanks also goes out to my fellow writers, Jeff Belanger and Thomas D'Agostino, who continue to support what I do and act as teachers and Tom's wife Arlene for her keen eye and her help on investigations. A special thanks goes to John Horrigan of the Massachusetts Monster Mash for keeping the spirit of the paranormal alive and Aaron Cadieux for getting it on film. I would also like to thank Mike Markowicz for challenging my ideas and helping to investigate the unknown, and Ann Kerrigan, his co-worker at East Bridgewater's Most Haunted. A special thanks goes out to the two families in Acushnet who allowed me and the investigators to share their house and their story, and to all the people who agreed to talk on the record and pointed me in the right direction, especially the sister from Taunton. I am grateful for the research help of Nicole Tourangeau and Dick Grant from Stonehill College, and Vicki Dawson from the Somerset Public Library. Jenna McFarland-Lord, who first started investigating with me, continues to be in my corner, and I thank her for that, along with my parents and family. As always, this book could not have been finished without the patience, understanding and encouragement of my beautiful wife and the twinkle in my son's eye.

Contents

Introduction.. 7

Preface: Travels Into the Weird 12

Part One: Where It All Began................................... 18
They See It All..20
It Happens First in Freetown 26
The Ghosts of the Wampanoags 39
Profile Rock • King Philip's Cave
Anawan Rock • Assawompset Pond

Part Two: The Legacy of State Mental Hospitals 51
The Hospital of the Insane...............................52
Just Down the Street 60
The Other Asylum 71

Part Three: Stories in Stone 78
Triangle Cemeteries 80
Riverside Cemetery • Broadway Street Cemetery
St. Stephen's Cemetery • Clark & Horr Cemetery
Oak Grove Cemetery • Ellis Bolles Cemetery
Mount Hope Cemetery
Remembering the Dead...90
The Cemeteries at the Apex 94
Palmer River Burial Ground • The Old Village Cemetery

Part Four: A Triangle Within the Triangle...................... 106
The Robinson Hauntings....................................108
The Hornbine School • Province Street
The Shade Factory
Massachusetts' Most Famous Ghost 117
The Other Most Famous Ghost...........................127

Part Five: In Session... 138
Walking the Halls..140
Fairhaven High School • Tabor Academy
Bridgewater State College
Wheaton Ghosts 146
Stonehill College 150

Part Six: Ghostly Cities, Places, & Objects 164
The Haunted City 166
The Summer Vacation.......................................172
The Haunted Violin 175
Friends and Bunnies 177
In the Bedroom...180
The Man in the Window 183
Don't Look too Much.......................................185

Part Seven: The Sounds of Ghosts 190
The EVP Guy...192
The Haunted Town Hall 198
The Children & Angry Old Woman......................201

Conclusion: And That's Only the Beginning.............. 217

Bibliography.. 219

Index.. 223

The Hoccomocco
aka The Bridgewater Triangle

The concept of the Bridgewater Triangle crept into my life like a black panther prowling the edge of the dark forest. I didn't go looking for it, but when I found it was there...it was hard to ignore.

I was gathering accounts from a specific area in Southeast Massachusetts that appeared to be a magnet for strangeness. The three Bridgewater's (Bridgewater, East Bridgewater, and West Bridgewater) formed a natural triangle, and I had been collecting some of the weirdest of reports, folklore, and tales from that area. I moved to the Boston area in 1975, and immediately was drawn to this part of the state by the unexplainable...the tangible intangibles I like to pursue.

In the early 1970s, I had written a column for *Fortean Times* in which I noted that Natives and later interlopers would often give names to places they found sinister or filled with unexplained phenomena; Anglo Europeans would often use the name "Devil." Historically, residents of such areas acknowledged the haunted or bedeviled nature of these places by giving them names such as Devil's Kitchen in Illinois, Devil's Den in New Hampshire, and, for the Spanish, Diablo Valley in California.

In recent times, areas of strange, unexplained activity—UFO sightings, mysterious disappearances, creature sightings, and a high incidence of accidents, violence, and crime—have been labeled "Triangles." The most famous of these is the "Bermuda Triangle." The term "Triangle" is now a commonly accepted way of describing what researchers of strange phenomena call a "gateway" or "window" area, that is, a location of focused unexplained activity. Northern Pennsylvania, in an area known as the "Coudersport Triangle," near the Black Forest, for example, is well known as one of these spots. The Black Forest is the site of giant Thunderbird reports, and the Coudersport Triangle supports all kinds of strangeness.

I noticed that something like that was going on in the large area surrounding the three Bridgewater's, mapped out in a broader area that I called the "Bridgewater Triangle." The name stuck. It seemed to be one of these focal areas and it made sense to use it to quickly explain what I was trying to say about the region.

The Bridgewater Triangle, by definition, includes the towns of Abington, Freetown, and Rehoboth at the angles of the triangle, and Brockton, Taunton, the Bridgewater's, Raynham, Mansfield, Norton, and Easton within the triangle. It covers an estimated two hundred square miles.

I wrote an article about the weirdness of the area, "The Bridgewater Triangle," for *Boston Magazine* in April 1980. Local media attention followed. Soon, I was being asked to talk to groups about the bizarre collection of sightings of creatures and unknown happenings. Reporters would write articles like "The Bridgewater Triangle: Some Light is Shed on Area Mysteries," for the *Brockton Daily Enterprise;* and *Evening Magazine* did a feature on the Triangle. Stories like this would especially appear around Halloween.

But for the residents of the area, and Natives too, the phenomena were year-round and centuries old. I kept investigating and soon learned that a "name game" clue had been right in front of me all the time.

The Bridgewater Triangle, I discovered, overlapped with a physical site, the Hockomock Swamp. The deeper I dug the more I found that the Hockomock area had always held its own share of strange occurrences. Because of its long history of evil, bedeviled, and ominous occurrences, the original Native residents had recognized this area for its strange and often sinister character.

I investigated the meaning of "Hockomock" and how widespread it is. I found it was the Algonquian word for the Devil — "Hockomock." There are at least ten places in the United States named "Hockomock"; six in Maine, two in

Massachusetts, one in New Jersey (Hockamik), and one in Minnesota (Hockamin Creek). It is the Hockomock Swamp that directly overlaps the Bridgewater (Massachusetts) Triangle. It is a place where people vanish and creatures like giant snakes, Bigfoot, Thunderbirds, and phantom panthers are seen.

I first talked to Hockomock-area residents and Native Americans about the meaning of the name "Hockomock" to discover its link to the word "Devil." Then I looked in a Depression-era Writers Project Administration (WPA) guide, the one titled, obviously, "Massachusetts," and found it defined the variant name for the swamp, "Hoccomocco," as "evil spirit." It was one of those "Eureka" moments. Of course, it was named "Hockomock," for it was a strange Fortean location named loosely after the Devil.

From the first edition of my book *Mysterious America* in 1983, until the newest completely revised and updated edition in 2007, I have written about the Bridgewater Triangle; of the lore, the reports, and of the danger that lurks therein. It is real to the people who venture in—as I have often.

We don't know what frightening experiences the Natives had to deal with, but they viewed the area as especially sacred and sometimes evil. Several years ago, an expedition of Massachusetts's archaeologists discovered an 8,000-year-old Indian burial site on Grassy Island in the Hockomock Swamp. The tale goes that when the graves were opened, the red ochre within the tombs allegedly bubbled and dissolved mysteriously, and every photograph taken of the site failed to develop.

On a site thirty miles up the Taunton River at the edge of the Hockomock Swamp, there is a mysterious forty-ton sandstone boulder that has been used by various mysterious nationalities (Egyptians, Phoenicians, Vikings, and Portuguese) as proof that they were the first "pilgrims." Dighton Rock, as it is called, sits on the riverbank directly across from the Grassy Island Indian burial grounds.

From colonial times comes the report of a "Yellow Day," when the skies above the area shone all day long with an eerie sulfurous yellow light.

In 1939, Roosevelt-era Civilian Conservation Corp workers, completing a project on King Phillip's Street at the edge of the swamp, reported seeing a huge snake "as large around and black as a stove-pipe." The snake coiled for a moment, raised its spade-like head and disappeared into the swamp. Local legends claim that a huge snake like this one appears every seven years in the Hoccomocco.

In 1971, Norton police sergeant Thomas Downy was driving along Winter Street in Mansfield toward his home in Easton. As he approached a place known locally as "Bird Hill" in Easton at the edge of the swamp, he was suddenly confronted by a tremendous winged creature over six feet tall with a wingspan of eight to twelve feet. It would appear that the officer with the feathery name experienced the Triangle's own version of Mothman.

In addition to legendary birdlike creatures, great cats— "lions" or "phantom panthers"—have been sighted regularly in places throughout the Bridgewater Triangle. In 1972, in Rehoboth, a "lion hunt" was organized by local police. Residents of the area had been terrorized by what they said was a large cat or mountain lion.

The Bridgewater Triangle has also had major flaps of UFO sightings in the 1970s. Radio talk show hosts were having so much fun with the reports, they joked about a busload of nuns disappearing in the Triangle. In more recent times, many reports of strange lights and noises in the sky above the massive power lines that run through the swamp have been recorded. Every January, "spook lights"—unexplained elusive balls of light—have been seen over the railroad tracks that run beside the Raynham Dog Track and through the swamp.

During the 1970s and 1980s, various sightings of Bigfoot, ranging from almost certain hoaxes to incidents involving eminently responsible witnesses and organized police hunts, have occurred. Farmers reported killed and mutilated pigs and sheep, and a night security guard at the Raynham Dog Track reported a series of horrible screams and screeches that frightened him and upset the dogs. Huge footprints, fifteen to eighteen inches long, were discovered in the snow south of Raynham.

Hounds of Hell have been seen here too. In 1976, a huge black "killer dog" was reported in Abington within the Bridgewater Triangle. The "dog" ripped out the throats of two ponies. Local firefighter Phillip Kane, the owner of the ponies, saw the "dog" standing over the bloody carcasses gnawing at their necks. He said that the "dog" eluded extensive police searches and, for a period of several weeks, terrorized the community.

In the Hockomock Swamp is Lake Nippenicket (locally called "The Nip"), a few miles northeast of Raynham. During the summer of 1980, several local men in a canoe on the Nip sighted a small, red-haired, chimpanzee-like ape that reportedly walked upright on the lake's island. When I interviewed them, they all sounded genuinely frightened and sincere.

In 1993, a series of reports of a "large, light tan cat the size of a great Dane," labeled "The Mansfield Mystery Cat," emerged from the area. Local officials took the sightings very seriously, especially after Fire Chief Edward Sliney had a mystery panther encounter of his own.

Strange human disappearances, ritualistic killings, and bizarre crimes have been reported in the Bridgewater Triangle in increasing numbers in the twenty-first century. Indeed, only the tip of the iceberg is known, and the sinister and mysterious nature of the Hoccomocco is to be revealed even more greatly in this book, *Ghosts of the Bridgewater Triangle*, Christopher Balzano's examination of the supernatural and paranormal events of the area.

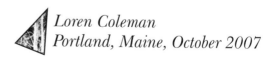

Loren Coleman
Portland, Maine, October 2007

Preface

Travels into the Weird

The unofficial entrance to the swamp.

I have been investigating the paranormal for more than fourteen years, which really means I have been collecting people's stories for that amount of time. For me there was no such term as "ghost hunter" back then. I heard a story, wrote it down, and went to the location trying to find out more information and to confirm what people said they had experienced. I read as much as I could on the subject, and I eventually came across Charles Turek Robinson's *The New England Ghost Files*. I had heard no publicity about it nor had I heard of the author before, but my friend bought it, and one night, when I had again been evacuated from my dormitory, *(which happened to be the haunted Charlesgate Hotel in Boston, but that is a story for another time)* a few friends went to her apartment down the street. Using dim candles and fading flashlights we read Robinson's stories, and I was hooked. It was not so much the hauntings themselves. There was enough in there to make anyone lose sleep, and I had heard many like them before, as I'm sure anyone in a rural New England town has. It was his style, his approach to telling someone's story that drew me in.

After noticing several of his stories involved locations in Rehoboth, Massachusetts, we headed out there one Halloween for what would be my first official investigation. We had cameras, flashlights, a photocopied map of the town on four sheets of paper, a Ouija board, and some incense. Oddly enough, we found no evidence of life after death that night. Shortly afterward, I launched Massachusetts Ghosts and Legends, now Massachusetts Paranormal Crossroads, and included the stories I had collected up to that point. I mentioned places all over the state, including previously unknown haunted places in Boston, Worcester, and Framingham. Then, of course, I posted my findings in Rehoboth, which originally consisted of stolen fragments of *The New England Ghost Files* and a few stories from our journey there.

I sat back and waited to see if more stories would come from people flocking to my site.

A strange thing began to happen. NO ONE wanted to share their stories from the North Shore or Boston. People were silent about Western Massachusetts and Cape Cod. Instead, what I began to get was report after report of hauntings from the Southeastern part of the state. The Red Headed Hitchhiker got some attention, but there were other stories trickling in about haunted cemeteries and little dark corners where phantoms were seen. They were a mixed batch. Some were teenagers who were scared of things they had seen, but also "responsible" citizens whose e-mails always began with, "I know you might think I'm crazy, but I have had something weird happen." The e-mails almost always asked me if I had heard of anything like that happening in their town, and after a few years I began to tell them I had.

Then a twist of fate occurred. As all good webmasters will tell you, one of the best ways to move up on all those search engines is to link to as many people as possible. I found Chris Pittman, the local authority on something called "the Bridgewater Triangle." I knew Chris because we had worked together in a restaurant for a while before either of us had started publishing our findings. As I read his research, my mouth dropped open.

The Bridgewater Triangle is an area of heightened paranormal activity noticed by the renowned cryptozoologist Loren Coleman. He had been doing research in the Bridgewater area and noticed a natural triangle between that town and East and West Bridgewater. As he began to draw the Triangle out, he found more cases until his research had stretched the region into a 200-square mile tract encompassing a dozen towns. He had mentioned his new name for it several times in the local media, but in his 1983 release, *Mysterious America*, now in its third edition, he brought the name to the masses.

I had been seeing his face for years talking about Bigfoot, but I had never read anything he had written. Going through *Mysterious America* was like finding part of an answer when you didn't even know there was a question. Using his book as a spark, I began to find out as much as a could about the Triangle. There were the reports of Bigfoot and Thunderbirds, but also of UFOs and black helicopters. There were demon dogs and balls of light, but I also found reports of ghosts increased in this same place. Southeastern Massachusetts seemed to be cursed.

It didn't stop at reports of the supernatural. The Triangle is home to more than a dozen asylums and mental health hospitals. While the majority of these buildings are abandoned and have a lore of their own, many were still active. Something was drawing in negative energy and inviting people who were the most likely to feed that power back to a source. There were heightened levels of suicide and mental health disorders. The reports I was hearing and the research I was doing told the same story I had been hearing from students I had talked to while working in the juvenile justice system.

Something was just plain bad.

There is a heightened level of crime in the Triangle's communities, not only in the large cities held within, but also the smaller countryside towns that would normally be labeled as quiet or sober. Freetown stuck out the most, but the criminal activity was being seen throughout.

I myself experienced manifestations of the curse while at the Triangle, which I passed off as coincidence when I took them as individual occurrences. There is rarely a time when I go there that something unexplained does not happen. One time while researching the Freetown forest for my first book I called my wife to tell her I would be home soon. She hung up the phone and slipped on the stairs, falling down the steep incline, and putting her foot through the glass of our front door. While taking a reporter on a tour of Bridgewater, I backed my car into a ditch and got stuck fifty feet from reported Bigfoot sightings for two hours. A few weeks later I was taking another group of reporters from Boston University on a tour of the Hockomock Swamp and was bit by a tick. I only discovered it days later because it had attached itself inside my bellybutton. It had to be removed by a doctor because it was in so deep, and I could only shrug when he told me to stay away from swamps and haunted places. In the summer of 2007 I traveled back to Freetown to do research on the Mad Trucker of Copicut Road and cracked my oil pan. The next day the car broke down at the intersection of Routes 93 and 95 near my house with my wife and son in the car and morning traffic flying by.

And, this is without even mentioning the time slips I have experienced while traveling on Route 79 late at night.

In the words of Alan Alves, a former detective from Freetown:

"If it's paranormal things or crime, it happens here before it happens in other places in the country."

His words rings true for everything from UFOs to suicide clusters.

And then there are the ghosts... The Triangle is the most haunted area in the state, and maybe all of New England. The stories Robinson had told only touched the surface of what people were experiencing there, and the stories take all forms. Some are passed down from generation to generation. Others are faint whispers told with a promise I would not share any names. Others are urban legends told as fact, disproved in part but with something unexplained at their root.

And, that brings me to the reason for writing this book. While there are some published accounts of ghosts inside the Bridgewater Triangle, there is no book devoted just to this extremely haunted place. There is no context for those stories townspeople have been passing among themselves for years. Studying ghosts, it's easy to want there to be a larger picture, to place random apparitions in a romantic painting of life after death or some kind of *other side* conspiracy theory. The Triangle doesn't need a writer's artistic license. The bigger picture is natural there.

I am always asked how it all began. What makes the land more haunted, more prone to oddities, and I have to shrug. Many point to King Philip's War, but I disagree. The Wampanoags were terrorized by dark spirits and unexplained tragedy well before the settlers arrived. I believe the war, and the horrific war crimes committed by both sides, was another symptom of the gloom that lives within the lines. I am left then to ask people smarter than I why they believe the Triangle is off.

Answers vary. Some say there is an energy rift that somehow allows different dimensions to reveal themselves, and they point to other places in the world where similar things happen. They can never tell me what started the rift, and I don't fully understand quantum physics. Others point to ley lines, or theoretical lines of energy underneath the surface of the earth that control magnetism and pull. Some claim the unique geological characteristics of the towns make it more susceptible to the paranormal. There is something about the water sources and the minerals in the rocks that attracts and magnifies the force. Again, the idea sounds good to me. We do not know what makes a ghost, no matter how many people state their opinions as fact, so a convergence of energy based on natural materials appeals to that side of us looking for a backbone for belief.

With no solid scientific proof that ghosts exist, there is little to support any reason for why one place may be more haunted than another. All we have is the stories of what people have experienced and the results of people who have been out there following up on the reports. The stories come quicker in Southeastern Massachusetts, and paranormal investigators have flocked there. They gather their evidence and share their experiences and become part of the tale writing itself in the Triangle.

I like to stick with what people have told me. First-hand evidence might be the best proof we have, and so I present these accounts as proof of a larger script being written in Southeastern Massachusetts. The Triangle has moved from a collection of stories to a story in and of itself, one that plays out through unsuspecting towns, and has everyday people as its characters.

Part One

Where It All Began

They See It All

I n late March and early April of 2007 Bridgewater made it into the national news. An inmate at Bridgewater State Hospital, who was there for evaluation and serving out a term for a minor charge, had committed suicide by hanging himself in the shower. The death pushed the Massachusetts state average for committed prisoners who killed themselves over twice the national average, but those high statistics are nothing new in an area where the general suicide rate is higher than the national average and where mental health is part of your mortgage closing. Death, like many unexplained things, finds its way into the Triangle.

Exploration of the Triangle can't begin without a nod to those non-ghostly things that make that part of the state their home. If there was just one issue, a sociologist could collect his or her information and come to a conclusion. What makes the area truly bizarre is the variety of things that make you scratch your head. It all starts with those BEASTS that defy characterization, and where the path it takes makes you want to stay west of Route 24.

Southeastern Massachusetts originally drew the eyes of investigators like Loren Coleman because of the odd animals that find their way there. The Wampanoags knew there was something unsettling there and avoided many of the darker places, like the Hockomock Swamp. There are ghosts who rule the Triangle, but not mentioning the other supernatural events is like watching the television with the sound off. The whole picture of the Triangle is what separates it from other haunted locations, and exposing the history is crucial to understanding just how tainted the land might be.

Everything in the Triangle begins with the Hockomock Swamp. The 5,000 acres of wetland has been home to some of the most disturbing accounts and encounters...ranging from

Bigfoot and Thunderbirds to UFOs. The history goes back much further than that. Even though the swamp was used as a base of operations during King Philip's War, the Natives avoided it. The name is said to translate to "dark place" or "place where spirits dwell" or as Coleman found out, "the devil's place." Other than a rail that has since been abandoned, there has been very little development of the land, making it home to all types of animals who have never been seen by civilization, except of course in small doses. Most who explore the wet terrain prefer to stay on the path or cut across a power line running perpendicular to it, and even those who dare not venture off the path and into the muck have reported feeling they were being watched or seeing shadows dashing through the woods, following them.

Giant birds, the size of humans, have been seen flying over the swamp. Their eyes are often said to be glowing red and they are known to track people the way chicken hawks fly over their prey. The same birds have been seen flying over the Raynham

The track in Raynham taken in the fall of 2007.
Notice the dark figure randomly picked up.

Track that borders the swamp. That is also the home of the Werewolf-like dogs who are much larger than the wild canines, wolves, and coyotes people sometimes see. Like the birds, their eyes have been said to glow red. Some say this is due to natural factors, such as headlights and flashlights reflecting off retinas, but some of the reports have occurred in the pitch dark with no light source to bounce off. There have never been any reported attacks of either animal, but...

Those who witnessed them knew they were in the presence of something not totally explainable.

The same cannot be said for the Bigfoot creatures that have been reported there and in other places in the Triangle. Many of the stories are from people who see...TALL, HAIRY ANIMALS running into the swamp and disappearing into the trees. Others are more up close experiences. One area of concern is Elm Street in Bridgewater. The mysterious beast has been seen there several times and might make the vast wooded area there his home. Sightings have included the street on the other side of the forest as well as the backyards that line the woods.

Unexplained animals exist throughout the Triangle, and the reports might feel isolated and exaggerated when taken on an individual basis. On September 22, 2005, a five-foot alligator was spotted in Abington. It was just one of four seen in the Triangle in a month's time. While these reports are explained away as the foolishness of people who try to keep the animals as pets, the reports have continued through the years. In 1988 there were several puma reports and in 1975 more black dog stories. In contrast, these animals are not being seen in towns surrounding Boston, Worcester, or Springfield—all major cities in the state with rural communities around them.

The news does not stop there. There have been sightings of UFOs all around the Triangle, including up and down RouteS 24 and 44, which are the backbone and shoulders of the Triangle. Of course, trends cycle up with the help of the media reports all around the country, but in the Bridgewater Triangle the sightings are much more common.

The experience is in the eye of the beholder, so it might not always be a UFO, even if there is such a thing, and all natural things can be explained away.

For example, there have been lights sighted over the swamp and the racetrack, and those who believe in aliens tend to believe they are UFOs and those who track ghosts translate them as spirits. Conspiracy theorists see them as government projects and aircrafts.

As the story goes, in 1908 a pair of undertakers headed toward Bridgewater saw what they referred to as a giant lantern and sat and watched the ball of light for over a half hour. Two crafts are said to have landed in Taunton in 1976. Police officers in Bridgewater have reported seeing lights in the sky they could not explain in 1984 and 1997. Another was seen at the Assonet Ledge, a hotbed of ghostly activity, in the 1960s. The reports are not always from the most respectable sources, and most cannot be confirmed, but like everything in the Triangle, the rumors persist and the shadows stay in the shadows.

All of this can be argued. Stories beget stories and legends fill in the gaps. The same cannot be said of the odd crime and the higher levels of suicide and mental health disorders. Many of the criminal reports come out of Freetown, a sleepy town where criminals come from miles around to dump bodies and do their misdeeds. The town has been at the center of drug and pornography rings and continues to be a magnet for cults whose actions are on record and whose activities sometime dip into murder.

All areas have crime, but there is such a thing as a disproportionate amount given the demographics and the size of each city and town. The first level is with the sheer amount of crime that draws national media attention. In addition to the multiple murders and the unsolved serial killer cases, there are also cases like the Big Dan rape case, which became the inspiration for the movie "The Accused" with Jodi Foster, and the killer who was discovered by an off-duty police officer at a rest stop along Route 24.

The other level is with the amount of violence involved in the cases. Lizzie Borden, or whoever killed her father and stepmother, massacred the victims beyond what would have been normal. In Freetown, a drifter was accused of being an undercover narcotics officer. Instead of just being killed, he was brought to the forest and lit on fire. The examples are too numerous to count, but perhaps the best example does not come from today's headlines, but rather from history books.

King Philip's War is often said to be the genesis of the negative energy in the Bridgewater Triangle, and there can be little doubt it contributes to many of the hauntings and horrific forces seen in the area. The crimes committed during the conflict may instead be a symptom of the problem. While most modern books write it off as a suppressed rebellion, it was in many ways the first war on our soil, and the atrocities on both sides were unusual given the past dealings between the settlers and the Native Americans and how each conducted warfare. Both killed innocent women and children and used hit and run tactics never before employed. Battles and raids were carried out as if the participants were possessed.

The devil may have come to Massachusetts. You cannot separate the word from its religious inference, but there is something dark there that is seen throughout the recorded history of the area. It is more than just a coincidence. It brands itself in the very names of the place and the attitude towards the land itself. Its history is a history of cycles, and the communities inside the Triangle are experiencing an active time.

Maybe that is what it comes down to. Many demonic cases hinge on the presence of an older tragedy. The emotions stirred up draws other bad things to it like a moth to a flame. That magnetism exists in the Triangle. In places like the swamp and the state forest you can feel it, often with an underlining good emotion trying to break through. With all that in the air, ghosts who might need that kind of juice to live again find it in abundance. Even the most seasoned investigator cannot say for sure what a ghost is, and every camp chimes in with their ideas and beliefs, but almost all have to do with energy and emotion. The towns within the Triangle have that to spare.

It Happens First in Freetown

W hen Loren Coleman began drawing the map for the Bridgewater Triangle, he stretched his lines by finding odd and unexplained cases. He stopped at Freetown because he had heard of some of the cult activity occurring there. It might seem arbitrary, especially given the odd things going on in the towns around it weren't included. PUTTING A PARANORMAL DOT ON THE TOWN SEEMED INSTEAD TO ACT AS FORESHADOWING.

Since the original publication of his book, Freetown has become one of the most touched areas in Massachusetts. The cult activity that had attracted Coleman may be in the forefront of people's minds, but scratching the surface away reveals some of the most disturbing tales of ghosts heard within the Triangle.

Freetown, located off Route 24, is like many rural towns in Massachusetts. There are dark, winding roads, often dropping off to dirt paths at a moment's notice. There is that typical misplaced feeling many towns in the area have. Historic buildings dating back before some states in other parts of the country are side by side with local fast food chains. Freetown might have something the others do not: *Of all the towns in the Triangle, it seems to be the most cursed.*

Satanic Activity

From the beginnings of English settlement, Freetown was off. It was the last major land purchase before King Philip's War and was sold in part to fulfill Massasoit's, the great sachem of the Wampanoags, drinking debts. It was signed by the man who eventually betrayed King Philip and whose death sparked the keg of war between the two cultures. Freetown was one of the battlegrounds of the war, and as the years passed, the lines were moved so that many of the towns in the area – Fairhaven,

Fall River, Tiverton, Rhode Island – all owe something to that original land purchase. It has also given birth or drawn in the darker elements that have become the embodiment of what the Triangle is.

Cults have been active in Freetown for over thirty years, but it is a small fraction of those who consider themselves Satanists that find the town that cause concern. Most are harmless, doing nothing more than trespassing or vandalizing. A few have gone to the next step, sacrificing animals such as birds and cows. Their marks are left all over the forest. At one time it was not uncommon to come across an upside down pentagram with a dead bird in the middle or a small voodoo doll pinned to a cross. Once a youth cut himself and wrote the Our Father in blood backwards on a poster board. He left it in the town's nativity scene after smearing the baby Jesus inside with blood. In the 1980s, a car of teens broke into a mausoleum, decapitated Angie Littlefield, and stole her head to use in a ceremony. In another incident a body was dug up twice and parts removed.

Some of the activity is much more sinister and is focused in the state forest there. In the 1990s a man walking through the woods came across a hidden bunker believed to have been used by a satanic group. Torn and stained clothes, mostly children's clothes, were found along with dolls with their eyes torn out. There was a small wooden chair, just large enough for a ten year old, and ritual weapons such as a knife. Something more serious was going on in the forest.

It had already been going on though. In 1978, a young girl named Mary Lou Arruda was found dead, bound to a tree in the forest. Although the method of death is still debated today, James Kater was eventually caught and tried for the murders. It took four trials and more than twenty years to finally send down a sentence. The reputation of the forest, and evidence found near the crime scene, allowed Kater to accuse a cult of the killings. Most who worked on the case doubt this, and some feel he might have been involved in one himself.

In the 1980s, a local pimp from Fall River was convicted of the murder of one of his employees. At least three dead prostitutes were connected to the case, and the media focused on Carl Drew as the leader of a satanic cult. He was painted as another Charles Manson, corrupting and ordering the murders. The group often used the woods for their ceremonies and had built a shack in the state forest. To this day Drew maintains his innocence, and he is actually backed up by people close to the case. Many feel the real leader, and one of the actual killers, was a young prostitute named Robin Murphy. She had turned against Drew and testified against him in return for a lesser sentence. She was released from jail in 2004. Many feel, however, even she was a bit player. A larger, more organized cult was manipulating the group, and it is this group, moving along the edge of the Triangle, that concerns police.

The cult may have also had a hand in the most infamous, unsolved murder case in Massachusetts. In 1988, the bodies of female drug users and prostitutes began showing up in the woods within the Triangle, the first of which was discovered in Freetown. In total, more than a dozen women were connected to the case, although many feel the count is much higher and that some of the bodies will never be found. Evidence in the case was ignored, mainly due to miscommunications, a misdirected task force, and personal vendettas and agendas. It also pointed to satanic cults and explained the ritual altars, upside down crosses, and odd drawings found at all of the crime scenes.

Following the activity of the cults is much like trying to grab hold of mist, but it still may be easier than trying to classify some of the supernatural creatures never mentioned in Coleman's original accounts of the Triangle. Their accounts read like the lineup of an old horror movie, but the stories are swapped and retold within the town. They may be the odd animals cryptozoologists look for, but there is something more ghostly about them. Some appear just on the other side of our world, and others ask for help from the other realm. All of them are the things nightmares are made of.

The Zombie

Zombies are the product of a good Hollywood script. For centuries the soulless creature was a common figure in cultures around the world, but the way we think of them today is more movie than myth. Zombies do not eat brains or travel in packs seeking revenge or flesh. More than the walking undead, these monsters are more likely the dead who do not know that they are actually still living. Southeastern Massachusetts has a large Portuguese population, and following natural immigration patterns, it attracts Portuguese-speaking people, especially Brazilians and Cape Verdeans. Both cultures have a strong link to voodoo and Santeria, forms of witchcraft originating in Africa and becoming mixed with Catholicism. Palo Mayombe is the negative side of these practices, and zombies are an integral element in the religion. Much like the practitioners in Haiti, priests or medicine men use natural, paralyzing drugs to convince the community someone has died. The priest then digs the person up and uses his power of suggestion to control the resurrected, convincing them their soul is now his. There are some who believe the art of making a zombie actually does steal the soul of the person, but even the hypnotic control of the priest is enough to convince the person he has been raised. This is then reinforced by the community who shuns the person as being cursed and refuses to go against the medicine man who has proven his abilities.

Freetown has its own walking dead. People have reported being chased by people whose eyes seemed vacant and who looked like they had been buried in the ground. With so many criminals finding their way to the forest, and so many victims being left among the trees, it might be easy to discredit the reports, but the people who see the zombies never use the word themselves. One woman ran into what she thought was a ghost along one of the walking trails in the woods. The man followed her at a steady pace, walking with a slight limp and covered in dirt. What convinced her something was amiss was the fact no sound could be heard from the man, even though he was breathing heavy and sliding his leg along the dirt, breaking branches in the roads.

Another time, a group of people walking in the woods one night came across a strange woman dressed in outdated clothes and so covered in dirt that it rose off of her in puffs as she approached them. Her eyes were described as lifeless and she never broke pace or spoke, even as they called to her and then ran back to their car. The experience was eerie enough for them all to leave the area; there were four of them, including two male members of the local sports team. But the zombie woman was not quite done with them...she followed them to the car, reached into the backseat, and attempted to pull one of the young men out with superhuman strength.

There have been reports like this in the forest throughout the years. While most never make it to the authorities, Detective Alan Alves, a former policeman from Freetown and an authority on cults and alternative religions, has heard them off the record. While his training as a detective tells him there is a sane explanation for the reports, his upbringing and the teachings of his Cape Verdean grandmother sometimes overrides his better judgment.

"I'm not sure what they are. They could be people drugged out, just hanging out in the woods. I know people do that. They could be people just trying to scare people. Some do that for fun or to cover up their little dirty deeds. I think there is a possibility they could be zombies. There's a lot of people doing things in that forest, and it wouldn't surprise me."

The Pukwudgie

Zombies can be a rational cause to make it easier to sleep, but there are other monsters in the trees. The most mysterious, and the most dangerous, come from a legend out of nearby Cape Cod. Their existence, and the fear and injury they can inflict, make them anything but words written on the page.

Pukwudgies have a long history in Southeastern Massachusetts and have been spotted in different places within and around the Triangle. They are two to three feet tall, troll-like creatures that have been described as having long, sometimes-canine noses and thick hair on their bodies. They are magicians, changing shape into different animals, such as dogs, birds, and insects. They use handheld weapons like arrows and sticks, but are also in possession of magical, poison dust. Their saddest weapons are the souls of those they have killed, and it is these souls they use to gather more.

Their history begins at the time the Wampanoags came to be in the area. They were under the supervision of a creator giant named Maushop who looked after them and made sure their mischief remained somewhat benign. When their actions would get too serious, or his wife, Quant, would nag him too much, he would catch as many as he could, shake them to cause disorientation, and then throw them to the corners of the known world. There was an uneasy balance between the tribe, the creator, and the little monsters.

One day Maushop was lured into the ocean by a mysterious woman. When he came back to land, he found the Pukwudgies had changed. Instead of being annoying, they had become evil, killing the Wampanoags, kidnapping their children, and setting fire to their villages. Maushop had put his five sons in charge when he left, but they had inherited his laziness and had let the Pukwudgies go unchecked. This angered Maushop, but it was not until he discovered they had also stolen his precious strawberry bread that he decided to do something about it. He and his sons hunted the monsters, but they were smarter

A rendition of a Pukwudgie drawn by Danielle Marte.

than the giants. They eventually killed all of Maushop's sons and attacked him. The legend becomes unclear at this point. Maushop either left Massachusetts because of his grief or was killed by the Pukwudgies. What is clear is that the creatures lived on, and appear throughout Wampanoag mythology.

The story of the Pukwudgies was preserved most recently in the children's book, *The Good Giants and the Bad Pukwudgies*, by Jean Fritz, but their adventures in the forest are anything but a pleasant bedtime story. They have been known to cause fires in the woods and attack people. They are said to control the spirits of the dead, and transform them into balls of light. People are drawn to these balls of light, and the Pukwudgies trail them to rocks or cliffs and crush them or push them over the cliff. There have been reports of something similar to the Pukwudgie from Maine to California, but the Freetown State Forest is home to several stories.

One woman saw what looked like a Pukwudgie while walking her dog in the woods. The dog, usually high strung and aggressive, cowered and then ran away. The woman could not classify what she had seen, but it later appeared at her window one night. It looked in on her, smiling, telling her it knew where she lived, and then ran away. A troubled young man once had something similar happen to him. He spotted the balls of light one night and was drawn into an overgrown part of the forest. He saw a little troll with long thick hair and ran away, only to find himself lost. He eventually found his way back to the trail, but a few nights later he was parked near the forest and saw the same troll smiling back at him through his side mirror.

Monster stories play with our imagination, but ghosts may be the true legacy of Freetown. Like the hitchhiker in Rehoboth, Freetown has its own haunted travelers—ones who might even have their own transportation. The legend has become known as the Mad Trucker of Copicut Road. The details and origins of the ghost are unknown and there is not much information about sightings. Those that have seen him, or people who know people who have seen him, describe a pickup truck that comes out of nowhere in the middle of the night. The truck pulls close behind your car, honking its horn while the driver sticks his head out the window and yells at you. The truck and driver then mysteriously disappear. Copicut Road itself is a dangerous road, alternating between pavement, dirt, and rocks. If something like the trucker story were to happen, it would be hard for a mortal man and his car to appear and then vanish on the road. The lack of stories to back up this legend makes it feel more like fiction.

What the Mad Trucker has going for him, however, is brethren in other parts of the forest. There are stories of road phantoms in at least three other locations in Freetown. In 1996, two men were driving down Slab Bridge Road near the forest. They drove over a man standing in the middle of the street. They heard and saw no impact, but stopped the car without pulling to the side of the road. There was no body or blood. They went back to the car, but the headlights turned on, blinked twice, and then shut off. The two men said the man was at least six feet tall with short hair and a dark shirt on.

Another driver claims she saw a man in the road on Bell Rock Road. She saw a man with short hair and a brown shirt in front of her car, holding his hands up as if bracing for an impact. The temperature in the car dropped as she drove through him, but when she stopped and checked for him, there was nothing there. Several other people say they know of the stories on Bell Rock Road, but the description of the man varies. He always has short hair, but sometimes he is dressed in a tuxedo or formalwear and one person even said the man was naked, lying in the road.

The Reservation

The most sacred part of the forest is the area known as the Reservation, a parcel of land within the woods off of Copicut Road set aside for the Wampanoags to use for ceremonies and gatherings. It is not in regular use, but when the tribe is there, it is a beehive of activity. Most of the time the Reservation is a solitary place with over-grown grass and wood and stone structures that look more like half broken down town fairground parts than a holy place. The welcome center is a boarded up wooden building with ancient refrigerators and air conditioners leaning up against it. The main ceremonial area is a cement floor with a small building attached, much like you would find at a small town's recreational center.

Despite its looks, the Reservation speaks to people who visit it and walk the grounds. While not all who go have a religious experience there, some have at least felt the presence of a positive higher power. One man described it as coming in from the rain after the heaviness of the forest surrounding it. Others have noticed a lack of sound, as if the birds have all flown away and the crickets have moved on. Cell phones have a habit of draining power or losing reception.

Some have seen or heard a tangible presence at the Reservation. In the summer of 2000 a man and his wife were near the visitor's center when they heard drums playing nearby. They followed the sound to the meeting place, noticing the drums getting louder and faster as they approached. When they reached the structure the sound continued, but there was no one there. They then witnessed five columns of dark smoke, about the weight of a person, floating in the corner.

People are often changed when they've been touched by the paranormal, and the Reservation has been known to turn people's lives around. One man was touched in the fall of 2004 when he heard a voice speak to him while he sat on the ground trying to meditate. He could not understand the words, but when he felt a strong hand on his shoulder, he closed his eyes, marveled at the fact he was alone, and changed the life he had been living—he quit his job for one closer to his heart and took a chance with a new relationship. Another woman felt the same way when she saw the ghost of a young boy walking in a nearby clearing. He was dragging his hand along the high grass, but when she called out to him, he turned, smiled, and disappeared before her eyes.

Native American ghosts have been seen in the state forest at the Reservation and in other areas of the woods. Given the strained relationship between the settlers and the Native Americans and the spiritual nature of some of the locations, this is not unusual. Most encounters are harmless and peaceful, but there is sometimes a twist that stays with the witnesses and drive them out of the woods.

On a path known as Breakneck Trail one man saw a jogger in front of him who looked very much like a Native American running without shoes. The jogger then began to levitate, continuing the same leg motion while hovering a few inches off the ground. The man stopped and the ghost stopped as well before vanishing. Many of the stories are like this: random encounters that touch the people who see them, but offer no answers to questions.

The Assonet Ledge

The most haunted stone area in Freetown is the Assonet Ledge. Nestled between Upper and Lower Ledge Road, it sticks out in a place that already stands out. The shear number of reports and different types of occurrences there place it in the elite group of supernatural locations in New England.

The Assonet Ledge — the most haunted location in Massachusetts.

The Ledge was the scene of tragedy. In the early 1900s, the site was used as a quarry and blacksmith shop; it blew up after some of the dynamite ignited. The explosion killed several men and forced the company to shut down production. Other horrible experiences are not as easy to document. According to rumors, and local authorities in the area, there have been at least a dozen suicides on the site, some unexplained and with witnesses. Even more disturbing are the off-the-record statements of law enforcement from Freetown. Some feel there may still be bodies buried under the surface of the water. No one knows for sure how deep it is, and the temperature has spoiled attempts by divers to reach the bottom on more than one occasion.

It seems there is a sadness trapped in the rock. People who go there feeling normal are struck by the sudden urge to jump from the jagged rocks to the cold, almost bottomless water below. The feeling comes as a heaviness or despair, and more than one person has been stopped before going over. The youth of the town often go there to drink and party, and it is another place in Freetown known for graffiti. People up there have seen images of people jumping off, or seen lights that appear to go over the edge into the water below without making a splash. They have felt the depression and have seen parties turn quickly when someone has reacted badly.

There is at least one ghost at the Ledge who has become somewhat of a celebrity. For decades people have spoken of the Lady of the Ledge, a scorned lover who is seen in the shadows near the edge and has even been seen jumping to her death. The story goes that she was set to meet her lover at the Assonet Ledge, but his family, not agreeing with their son's choice of lover, kept him. The Lady, feeling her beloved had abandoned her, jumped rather than live another day without him.

It is a classic urban legend, but in this case the back-story might have been added to explain the actual ghost people were seeing. There have been suicides, and people have seen the woman, dressed all in black or looking like a shadow. It might only be romantic fiction used to make sense of her meaningless death.

People believe that the Pukwudgies have a hand in the hauntings at the Ledge. It is known that they often lured people to rocks and cliffs and then pushed them over. While no one has ever spotted a creature at the spot, orbs and flashes of light, typical traits of the Pukwudgie, are often seen. One woman saw a large ball of light while standing close to the edge. It got bigger as it reached the surface of water and then sunk, as if something was pulling it back down. The translucent images of Native Americans have been seen at the Ledge as well. While the quarry did not exist as it currently appears now during the days of the Wampanoags, it might still have their energy trapped there. At least two people have seen figures climbing down the face of the rock, only to disappear when called to. Several have also witnessed what looked like a Wampanoag jumping from the top and vanishing before hitting the water.

The location may well be designed to draw the negative energy that has made its home there. The odd mix of granite, feldspar and hornblende, and running water might make for a natural setting for the paranormal. While the mix of natural elements while exploring ghosts is only a theory, much of the activity in the Bridgewater Triangle, just like at the Assonet Ledge, can be linked to this. In addition to collecting or magnifying ghosts, religions that focus on energy feel the power of the Ledge. Like with many places throughout the forest, the Ledge has been known to be the site of Wiccan rituals and satanic activity.

The why of the ghosts of Freetown may never be answered. There have been too many bad things that have happened there, and so much misfortune to trace it back. It feeds itself though, like perpetual motion. Some Native Americans have said the area will be cursed until it is all given back to the Wampanoags, but this is not the view of the whole tribe and too easy an explanation.

There are ghosts and monsters in Freetown that make us rethink the way we see the natural world.

There is crime, unsolved and left open after decades, and misery growing up like a tree with its roots in the past. The why may never be revealed, but the townspeople know the questions...like a story passed down through generations.

The Ghosts of the Wampanoag

The most common answer given when people ask why the Triangle is haunted is the brutality that happened during King Philip's War. It would seem to be an excellent source for any kind of haunting. The negative emotions the war brought out on both sides and the number of innocent people quickly murdered would make the perfect backdrop for any type of paranormal activity. Add to this the number of Wampanoag burial grounds in the area that predate the arrival of the settlers, and the makeshift ones created to bury the dead of the war, and the number of spectral sightings has the potential to go up. Some say the land is cursed because of the war, the taking of land, and the destruction of the Natives' culture.

Many of the legends and Native American hauntings have to do with the Wampanoag royal family, or the children of Massasoit. They were the generation in control when the war broke out, and English settlers' archetype for what an Indian was. Today, we are still obsessed with the culture and the characters that shaped those early days of America. In addition to the campus of Stonehill and several highways, the descendents of Massasoit are said to haunt several places inside the Triangle. These ghosts might not be who we think they are, but they are true ghost stories nonetheless.

Profile Rock

It all starts with the ghost people have reported in Freetown. The most famous spot in Freetown may also be one of its most haunted. "Old Joshua Mountain" has gained a more cosmetic name over the years and one that hints at the origins of the ghosts there. Profile Rock is located across the street from the

Profile Rock. *Courtesy of Jeff Belanger and ghostvillage.com.*

main forest on Slab Brides Road, but is under the jurisdiction of the rangers there. People from all over the state, and all over New England, come to see the perfectly preserved face found naturally there. It is Massachusetts' Old Man in the Mountain, and as of late it seems to be faring well. Although historically known as a place to party and for vandalism, the nose of the face in the stone now has a retaining bar to keep its good looks intact.

The face is believed to be that of Massasoit, the leader of the Wampanoags during the arrival of the Pilgrims in Plymouth, but the spirit trapped there might be his son, Philip. It is said Profile Rock was considered a sacred place to the Wampanoags, used to meet and discuss important matters in the tribe. The rock itself acted as a lookout, especially during the war.

Its resemblance to Massasoit may have attracted Philip to it during the dark days of the war. He might have felt some connection to it, as if he could channel his father's advice and guidance by being at it. It is also said he was there the night before he died and that he knew of his fate. The grief he released praying and meditating there that night somehow left his energy in the stone, and many believe you can still see him on the rock today, seeking counsel and consolation. There have been several reports of seeing a man on top of Profile Rock sitting with his legs crossed and his eyes closed. The man disappears while the observer watches. He has also been seen standing on the stone, looking out and then fading. This happens most often during sunset. Ghostly lights, mainly white and green, have also been spotted at the top of the rock.

"Just some guy on the rock," remembers Richard of his experience in late 2002. "They clean the rock and make it look nice, but the kids always find their way back. I go there to relax, and sometimes I see a guy on the rock. He just sits there, but when I turn away, he's gone. Now come on. This guy is a ghost, but I've seen him five times."

On that one day, Richard had brought his bike up the path because he did not want to leave it in the nearby parking lot. He walked it up the trail and saw the man on the rock again.

"I had gotten used to him, so it was no big deal. But this time, he turned to look at me. He was too far away for me to see any detail, but I could tell he was looking at me. He jumped from the top and I never saw him hit (bottom). There was no impact, no fading away or anything. He just jumped and was gone."

Richard dropped his bike and ran down the path, convinced it was a real person. There was no one there, and despite the fact the ghost had jumped toward where Richard was standing, he was not seen leaving the area or climbing out of the rock. That was the last time Richard saw the man; he's now convinced Philip no longer wants to be seen.

Anawan Rock

Most of the Native American ghost stories heard in New England are quick glimpses of something unknown, over before they can be thought about. Most are peaceful. However, there is another type of haunting where the spirit is not so happy to see you. Whether it is leftover guilt for colonial injustices or a misunderstanding of the culture, angry Indian ghosts are everywhere, and when no reason can be found for the disturbance, people fall back on the classic "Ancient Indian Burial Ground" excuse. Even in places where the Native American culture was once dominant, the reason is often a shot in the dark.

The hauntings at Anawan Rock, off Route 44, are more than just an educated guess. If a Native American spirit should haunt any place, it would be here where the ultimate betrayal played itself out. The closing days of King Philip's War were bleak for the Wampanoags. Philip was dead, killed by one of his lieutenants he had wronged, and his war general, Anawan, was left to try and win the war or negotiate peace. Their final surrender was at a rock in Rehoboth where Captain Benjamin Church promised fair treatment for the agreement that would end the war. Once they were removed and shipped to Plymouth, Church's orders were trumped and the band of Wampanoags were beheaded. Taken at the same time was a special belt of wampum's that held the history of the people, the closest thing they had to a written history. It is said Philip gave the belt to Anawan at Profile Rock before his death, and according to Charles Robinson, there are records Church received the belt. Much like the vow made to the Native Americans that day, the belt and the tribe's link to their past vanished.

The rock is not much to look at now. Often covered with graffiti, the rock was described by one person as a place where a dump truck had just emptied out its load. Others find the stone beautiful and the surrounding woods a peaceful place to go. The general sense is the rock likes some people, but wants others to leave and never come back. It is not the granite that decides, but the ghosts that live there. Investigators and sightseers, inspired by the tales told in Robinson's book, have gone there to experience their own taste of activity—and many are not disappointed. They join the residents of the town who have known the place was haunted for years.

"It's the fires that do it for me," says Tom, a local resident who has read the book, but began going there long before that.

Anawan Rock

"I first went there because of the history. You know, somewhere famous in our town. People forget that war, even in this area, but not me. I like history."

The first time he went he was unimpressed by the rock itself and said the air had a dirty smell to it. "Like garbage, but not. Then there was the electric smell. A thunderstorm smell. That's when I noticed the fire."

Tom remembers there was a fire at the base of the stone, maybe ten feet from him. He watched as it grew bigger despite the fact it made no sound and gave off no heat. He says it got larger and then faded away.

"It didn't put itself out or smother. It vanished, like when a movie fades in and out. I don't know what it was, but I keep coming back expecting to see it again."

Tom is not a paranormal investigator, but enjoys the scene for its natural beauty and for the rush he gets as he waits for the next fire.

"I've been there a hundred times. Each time I look for fire, but nothing. Sometimes I see something out of the corner of my eye. I know the woods, so I don't think it's anything natural. Supernatural, I don't know."

Fires have been seen all over the Triangle, usually in places with some connection to Native American culture. There is really no reason for these fires to appear unless they have some older, now forgotten meaning to the spirits who remain. They never try to burn or touch the witness and they happen often enough that local firefighters joke about them.

"I love that place. I always get evidence from there," says Luann, a local paranormal investigator from New Bedford who founded Whaling City Ghosts after years of having unexplained experiences in her house. She has been to several places in Rehoboth, but finds Anawan Rock to be the most active. She went there once as part of a special radio broadcast for "Spooky Southcoast," a local show that features paranormal topics and guests. She went to several places that night, reporting her findings live on the air, but it was the stone she felt most connected to. She feels the area wants her there. "I think they know I'm part Native American. They can sense that and they like that I'm there."

That night her partner recorded all types of activity. "Soon after arriving, we began to hear swishing noises in the forest around us. As time progressed, it seemed as if they were pants, swishing together, as figures flitted behind trees. I did not mention this feeling, but then my partner related to me, and I agreed." In addition to the sound, Luann reported seeing other figures in the dark.

"At one point, as I turned from snapping shots where I'd heard the swishing noise again, I thought there was a tall, thin, older Indian man standing against a tree. He was grey and wrapped in a blanket or fur, but then he vanished so fast, I wasn't sure I'd seen him, I was not quick enough to catch him with my camera, he was that quick. At one point an unseen hand touched the woman she was out with."

These sightings are not common for the location, but Luann heard the noises reported by others who've been to the rock. Many people report hearing drums being played, chanting, or words being called out, usually not understood because of the language people hear it in. The most famous quote, written about in *The New England Ghost Files* and then repeated by others near Anawan Rock, is a man yelling "Iootash, Iootash," which is Algonquin for, "stand and fight." Luann heard another conversation.

"I had learned a bit of Wampanoag for the occasion, and had related some words to Gabby, my partner for Whaling City Ghosts. 'Neetomp' was to me the most important word we could know with possibly hostile Indian spirits. It means friend. The Wampanoag language is extremely difficult, so I only learned simple words and may not have been using them in proper context, or pronouncing them correctly. As we moved about we repeated the word 'Neetomp' many times, we wanted them to know we were friends." As they left the woods, they recorded an unseen voice repeating "Neetomp." In addition, they also recorded someone saying the word "Kinsman" in Algonquin.

Other people's experiences might not be as dramatic, but the feeling is much the same. Justin, another investigator, says:

"Something is definitely watching you in there. I've tried to get any piece of evidence I could, but all I can say is there's something watching you. You hear these deep voices, but I can never record them."

Anawan Rock is part of our history. It does not point to a pleasant time in this country's history, but the stone does not lie.

King Philip's Cave

During the dark days of the war, Philip was known to hide out in several places throughout Southern New England in an attempt to be the figurehead of his people and a symbol of hope to rally behind. Until his betrayal, he was a hard man to catch, and many of his hideouts are said to still have a bit of him left there.

One such place is King Philip's Cave, located in the Rocky Woods, off Route 44, in Taunton, Massachusetts. The opening of the cave is said to be large enough for the soldier and his horse, and over the years people have seen a green glowing figure walking near it. Edward Lodi, a local writer who records ghost stories and uses local history as a basis for his fiction, wrote of it in his book, *Ghosts from King Philip's War*, but did not touch upon the sightings.

Brian tells his story second-hand, but other people, also telling the stories as something they only heard about, have backed up several of the details.

"The place is haunted. No one has ever seen anything in the cave, but the vicinity has a ghost people talk about. There is a green man who is seen walking nearby. People say it is an Indian. He is a light green, but glowing and not all there. He seems to be in a hurry and walks real quickly, like he is trying not to be

noticed. Dozens of people have seen him. When he notices he is being looked at, he dissolves away into nothing. But there is one person who was attacked. The ghost started to dissolve, but then ran towards the guy. He never made it there, but the guy was close to insane after that."

The cave and its entrance has been the victim of modern construction, but the stories still remain.

The Man in the Swamp

In the same book, Lodi provides a possible reason for an odd haunting at the racetrack and the Hockomock Swamp. He writes how someone approached him during a book signing in Raynham who wanted to discuss the hauntings in the town. She claimed Philip was looking for his head there and was roaming the afterlife in search of the one thing he needed to make his body whole. According to his research, Lodi discovered the area was basically left untouched during the war because of allegiance and respect for the Wampanoag leader. This seemed to back up the claims that somehow his head had made its way to Raynham.

Whether this is true or not, there have been ghostly Native Americans sighted at the track and in the swamp. One of the most convincing stories comes from Dean, who has spent "too much" time at the track. Several years ago he spent a good part of the day, and a large amount of his paycheck, there and left well after the sun had set. He had a twenty-minute ride home, and as he pulled out, he felt the urge to relieve himself. He saw no harm in pulling over near the entrance and getting it done right there.

"I was facing the woods, right into the swamp, and I saw this guy. It was chilly, but not really cold, but this guy was almost naked. He was walking into the woods. He looked like an Indian to me. I shouted out to him to tell him things were pretty hairy in there. He turned around with this angry look, shook his fist at me, and then kept walking. I looked away for a second, and he was gone. There is no way he could have gone in the trees without me seeing. I wasn't looking for a second."

Angel was riding his all-terrain vehicle through the swamp when he saw what he believes was the ghost of Philip. His story sounds like a classic road haunting, but it takes place in one of the most high-energy places in the United States. He was riding along when he saw someone walking in the road in front of him. He was wearing what looked like tan shorts and had short, black hair. "He was over enough that I didn't have to stop and he didn't have to move. I wouldn't even remember it if I didn't see the same guy maybe ten minutes later. He was walking on the side of the road again, but this time he frowned at me when I passed. The first time he ignored me."

Five minutes later, as Angel was thinking of how he would phrase the story to his friends, he saw the man again. "This time he was in the middle of the road. He came out of nowhere and I hit him. I saw a flash and then nothing. I whipped out, but he wasn't there anymore." Angel says he was shaken by the experience and has not ridden nearby since. He also says he saw a picture of Philip in a book and recognized him as the man he saw in the swamp.

Assawompset Pond

The war was sparked by the execution of three convicted murderers by the British. The men were accused of killing John Sassamon, a rival of Philip's and a man known as a Praying Indian, or a Wampanoag who had converted to Christianity. His body was discovered in Assawompset Pond, off Route 10S in Lakeville and Middleboro, after he had made threats to Philip and openly accused him in court of crimes against Plymouth colony.

His ghost is said to still haunt the pond. He comes out in winter, and is seen walking across the frozen surface. Page saw him during the winter of 1989, and although she is not sure it was Sassamon, she knows what she saw was a ghost.

"I was on the bank because my friend lived close by. We had been sledding and were just fooling around. I was twelve at the time, but I know what I saw. A man came out of the ice and walked ten feet away from me. When he reached a certain point, he sunk back in, like something had pushed him in."

The murder might not be playing itself in modern times, but there is something unusual happening on the water. It is said to be the resting place of Maushop and his wife, and tales connected with it also place many of the Pukwudgies there. The stories make it out to be the burial place of hundreds of them who died during the final fight between the giants and the little ones.

Kenny remembers seeing the lights, although he had never heard of a Pukwudgie before. "They were like fireflies, but much bigger. They were each about the size of a baseball and they floated in the air and then dove back towards the water. Twice I sat there and watched them, and my friend said they looked like car headlights. That's fine, but headlights don't move like that and I was close enough to see them in three dimensions."

The fog that rolls off the pond is said to be Maushop's pipe smoke, but Kenny experienced something much more sinister. "It was about in the middle of the water…this thick white smoke that moved like a person. I tried to point it out to my friend, but when I called out it seemed to turn around and come towards me. I ran as fast as I could back to my house."

Part Two

The Legacy
of State Mental Hospitals

The Hospital of the Insane

The Taunton State Hospital. *Courtesy of Sally Ashton Forrest and the Booo group.*

Although not as famous as its coastal brother Boston, Taunton is the largest city in term of square mileage in Massachusetts. With one foot firmly placed in Massachusetts and the other straining towards Rhode Island, it is very much a city of two personalities. Rural areas quickly drop off into a more urban setting, and people whisper about ghosts on stoops and storefronts. Like many of the surrounding towns, it has a strong history of haunted buildings and cemeteries, but Taunton's real terror emanates from its decaying asylum, a symbol of Massachusetts' desire to conserve its stone palaces and a representation of how it never quite got it right.

Taunton State Hospital first opened in 1854 to alleviate the strain felt by the state hospital in Worcester. Like many of the asylums built in Massachusetts, its architect, Elbridge Boyden, based his design for the building on the revolutionary ideas of Dr. Thomas Kirkbride who had begun to inspire some of the most beneficial institutes in the country, most of which are now said to be haunted. Kirkbride's legacy seems to be his knack for... CREATING BUILDINGS THAT TRAP SPIRITS AND ATTRACT PARANORMAL ADVENTURE SEEKERS. His flagship, Danvers State Hospital, is widely considered the most haunted building in Massachusetts, and the number of structures in the state thought to be haunted within the Triangle has led to rumors of Kirkbride's involvement in the occult.

The concept of the hospital was to build a place where patients could experience a rural setting and fresh air and to allow them to use the grounds of the facility for such occupational therapies as working the land and growing crops. It was revolutionary in its day. Instead of darkened rooms emanating whispered cries, patients were encouraged to heal by reaching out and reconnecting with the natural world. The 132.5-acre plot of land, with several small bodies of water, seemed perfect. The design of the main building itself was created to have a centralized administrative section and a nurse's station that could then be dispatched into the hospital through legs off the main building, with the worse patients being at the end of each leg.

The hospital itself consisted of fifteen buildings, few of which are still in use. Its history tracks the ideas and attitudes towards mental health over the past century and a half. Over the years it was always on the cutting edge of experimentation. In the 1870s, the doctors submerged patients in water tanks and then subjected them to extreme cold in an effort to jolt them out of their ailments. In the first half of the twentieth century, frontal lobotomies were popular. In the second half, electric shock therapy became popular and, over the next few decades, thousands of patients received high doses of electricity in an attempt to rewire something broken but not fully understood.

The hospital's clientele through the years was diverse, and the nature of the sick varied. Its most famous resident arrived in 1892 when Lizzie Borden was held there for several days following her arrest for the murder of her parents in their Fall River home. Although she was acquitted of the crime, her place in history was sealed. It is rumored a doctor at the hospital examined her and declared her to be insane, although no record of the meeting exists and the evidence was not brought up at her trial.

The majority of the buildings closed in 1978 due to construction flaws and rumors of abuse and neglect. In addition to housing several administrative departments for the state, the hospital served for years as a secure lockup and mental health facility used by Massachusetts' Department of Youth Services, Department of Social Services, and the Department of Mental Health. It housed convicted juvenile offenders and offered care to wards of the state and the youth of Massachusetts with specific and nonspecific mental health issues and a history of violent behavior. While it was a far cry from the horrors seen at the height of its capacity, the modern hospital still made employees uneasy. In 2004, a report was released that claimed ninety-seven percent of staff at the hospital claimed dangerous conditions there risked the safety of patients and staff and that many had considered leaving because of the state of the facility.

Though she has since left, Leslie said in 2005 while still an employee there:

> *"I hear the stories about the ghost. I don't know about that. It's possible and nothing in that place would surprise me. I just don't feel safe there. Maybe it's the same in all these places, but I get uneasy. At night there is sometimes a silence that makes me want to hum to break it up. Other times I feel the place is going to explode because there is so much juice."*

The hospital has changed its name several times over the years, always in compliance with the attitude of the era towards mental health, but it was one of its most recent nicknames, Taunton Secure, that added to the intimidating presence and created fear among the residents and staff. Anyone who has spent time there, on either side of the glass, has been touched, but unlike other hospitals and prisons in the state, the victims speak freely.

The ghosts that live there are hard to track down. They are a varied collection, making a statement about the misery that was suffered on the grounds for decades. Memory rests on top of memory on top of grief there, and those who believe tragedy breeds negative energy that can remain in a place need only walk near the building to have their argument reinforced.

The grounds and the architecture of the buildings have been described as Gothic and beautiful, but the whole property is now off limits to the people with cameras that used to stroll the area and run road races across its lawn. Once, it did attract locals. It was a place to relax and enjoy a touch of nature. There were even tours of the grounds to encourage the people to accept the stone and steel structure.

"The place is beautiful," says Sara, a longtime resident of Taunton. "Or it was. It looks like it feels now. Growing up down the street we loved to walk around by there. But there were places that just felt wrong. We would walk and then look at each other and want to leave. The place is evil."

Stacy felt the same way about the grounds. It changed quickly for her as well, especially at night. "I remember one night I drove through the hospital grounds during a full moon and some of the patients were screaming in the night. Very spooky place." Although she never experienced anything, she admits she kept her distance when the odd feelings would come on.

Residents in town echo the sentiment. Taunton State Hospital inspires those kinds of feelings in people. Older residents remember the beauty of the place, while others remember hearing screams from down the street, even after the main buildings were closed. Many see it as a negative mark against the town.

Mark lived in the town for over thirty years, but now lives in the other side of the state. "I'd see lights over the place. I'm not willing to say it was a ghost or something cause I don't know about that stuff. I just got sick of people telling me my town was haunted or weird. They'd hear I was from Taunton and the first thing they'd want to know about was the hospital. It's what the people in this state know about us."

The reputation of the hospital has changed over the years. It shifted from the place where the insane people were to the place were the ghosts haunted. No one can remember when the stories began, but they have now taken on a life of their own. Ask for a list of haunted places in Massachusetts, and the grounds of Taunton always come up. Its legacy remains in the realm of Danvers and Met State, and of all the old asylums, more people have stories from Taunton.

It is not just an old haunted asylum...it's a place people still remember seeing things they could not explain.

The grounds, once cherished and enjoyed, are the subject of many of the stories. Long before it closed, people saw things they could not explain. Spirits are said to walk outside the building, often seen as mist or dark clouds. Reports come in of an elderly man crouching and stroking the grass. He wears simple clothes, usually said to be jeans and a dark shirt, making him seem more like a former employee than a patient. When approached, he smiles and disappears. Others have seen people in light pants and white shirts. While pictures of the people who made Taunton its home are hard to come by, some feel, at least by stereotype, these souls are those of former residents. Many of the stories that come from the hospital read like horror, but many who lived there had their best, clearest days involved with the occupational therapy Taunton offered. This positive energy might also survive. It seems those who sought comfort in the hospital and received it still find their way back.

Other ghosts seen on the grounds are not so friendly. In a cemetery on the property one resident had an experience that changed his life. As a juvenile from the area arrested on drug charges, he was serving a stretch before leaving for a residential treatment facility. He was able to find a way out of the building and decided to hide in the cemetery to lay low and plan where he would spend the night. As he crouched near a tombstone he felt cold hands on his shoulder. Thinking he had been caught, he raised his arms and turned around. There was no one there but he heard a faint voice whisper the word, "Leave." He walked back to the building barely able to breathe and turned himself in.

While the youth readily believed his story to be true, some of the details might have been blurred due to his drug use and the excitement of his escape. According to the Danvers State Memorial Committee, an organization closely monitoring abandoned asylums and cemeteries in Massachusetts, there is no graveyard on the grounds. They report evidence of women patients sewing clothes for the deceased there, but claim most were buried in pauper graves in nearby locations, including the Mayflower Hill Cemetery. Other burial grounds have been sited near the hospital, and he may have been further away from the building than he originally thought.

Taunton State Hospital is more famous for the ghosts that stay inside the building. During its days as an asylum for the insane, there were rumors of cult activity at the hospital. Some even say this caused its initial closing, although that has never been confirmed. Staff members would bring their more incapacitated patient down into the basement to conduct bizarre rituals to Satan. The stories even tell of several patients sacrificed and the appearance of the Devil himself. Regardless of the rumors, parts of the basement had unexplained markings on the walls for decades. Places like Taunton are mills for urban legends, and the story seems fantastical. What lends credibility to these stories are the numerous accounts of people who have gone into the basement and reported seeing the graffiti and having their own supernatural experience. Staff, uninformed about the stories of what had happened there, speak of cold spots that moved with them whenever they were down there. Some saw a scuffling shadow or a ball of light that disappeared as if walking through the wall.

Jacky saw a fog in the basement and left soon after. "They told me it was my imagination. They said it was an old place.

The people that actually worked there, you know, worked for a living, said it was a ghost or something. I saw that smoky man down there twice, and the second time I quit. It wasn't worth it." Jacky says the smoky man was a little over five feet tall and consisted of a dark, solid haze, in the form of a person. She was never able to see it dead on, but both times saw it dash in front of her as she moved along the floor.

One staff member claimed he reached the final step only to feel himself stop. He closed his eyes and felt as if he were experiencing the awful things that had happened there in vivid detail.

"I heard and saw everything. I could smell smoke. I heard a drum playing and weird chanting, like devil worshipers." He took a step back and was back on the stairs and the scene flashed away instantaneously. He quit the next day and still has trouble describing what he saw in detail. "I don't even want to think about it, but I have nightmares. I only tell of what happened because it might make them go away."

The evil does not stay in the basement though. Screams are heard from the areas where the electric shock treatments and cold therapies were conducted. Residents have had their lights turn on and off in the middle of the night. The abandoned or burnt down sections have rooms that are illuminated by light, although there are no working lights in those buildings. Some have even seen small children and disheveled adults peer down at them from a place people are not supposed to still be in.

Many have also experienced a shadowy man who appears out of nowhere. At times he is not much more than a shadow having no specific form and moving as if crawling across the wall. Other times he is more solid although somewhat stretched out. Three things remain constant in the report however; his face can never be seen, he is always described as being male, and he appears in the corner of the resident's room in the middle of the night and stands as if watching them.

Shadow people are a newer theme in paranormal investigating, and the reports of these dark figures have been gaining momentum. In normal circumstances there is very little interaction with people, as they tend to make their presence known as spots in the corner of the witness' eye. These ghosts might be something more. They are frequently seen in areas of the Triangle, but almost always in cases where there has been another haunting. Theories abound about what they might be, and many in the field believe they are the mark of a demonic presence. They seem to feed off energy, be it from a resident or a patient at a hospital like Taunton, or a ghost or spirit left behind.

In March 2006, the main building suffered one of the largest fires in the state's history, one of many the hospital has endured over the years. Although no one was hurt, more than one hundred firefighters from eighteen departments were needed to finally bring the fire down. The main building — the source of most of the haunted stories — was destroyed beyond repair, leaving the future of the entire hospital up in the air. Early reports claim the fire was set, but who caused the final blow to one of Massachusetts' most notorious haunts will probably never be determined.

Since the beginning of 2002 these fires have happened in many of the asylums and hospitals throughout Massachusetts, and their explanation runs the gamut of the supernatural as well as inspiring the thoughts of conspiracy theorists. Some believe the energy left in these places has enough power to spark and cause a fire. Others feel that the buildings, which are often abandoned, are perfect targets for arsonists or troublemakers. Still some feel companies looking to develop the land have set the fires to force the people out or to lower the price of the land.

The future is up in the air for the old hospital for the insane. People continue to come forward with their stories, talking about the days when patients talked to the wall, and uncomfortable staff pretended it meant nothing. In the Triangle the future is always uncertain, but one thing remains constant:

Things in Southeastern Massachusetts have a habit of not staying dead and buried, and no matter what the hospital becomes, you can be sure a part of what it once was will rise again to remind the next generation of what once happened there.

Just Down the Street

T aunton may be known for its haunted hospital, but the ghosts there might leave the grounds and find their way into the homes of the people in the neighborhood. Many have experienced odd shadows or heard unexplained noises, but one family's experience went well beyond bumps in the night. For them there was something dark touching their lives, and two sisters separated by years and ideas, both believe what they experienced was born in the buildings down the street. Something dark walked off the grounds and into their lives.

Valerie's family moved to Hodges Avenue in Taunton when she was eleven years old. She was within walking distance of the hospital and remembers often driving through the property as a shortcut to the other side of the town in the 1960s. She is the oldest of three sisters, all of whom had experiences in the house. The house has had major changes through the years, but the bad feelings remain. She now lives across the country, and although her family is no longer renting the house where she experienced her haunting, her memories of those nights remain part of the reason she does not wish to return to Massachusetts.

The house on Hodges Avenue looks very different than it did back then. The brick that now frames the front was once wood, with polished woodwork inside. There were hedges and a lilac tree instead of the bare lawn that now blends into the house next to it. When the owner died, the building was bought by a family who chopped all the trees down and put up chain-link fences. They got rid of the lilac tree and the hedges and made it what it is today. The cosmetic difference might have been enough to shift the negative energy, but that does not change the sisters' memories, many of which still wake them up today.

The experiences that happened inside on the third floor of the house still resonates with them. About a year after they moved in, one of the younger sisters had started to hear weird noises outside the house a few nights before she woke Valerie up to confirm it. She had not yet shared it with her older sister, but that night she had had enough. She was finally able to get Valerie up, and told her what had been keeping her up nights. Valerie heard it too. Although she cannot remember the time of night it happened, she remembers with detail the sights and sounds.

"I could hear what sounded like metal banging on metal. It seemed normal at first, but after a couple of minutes, I realized it was too weird. Who would be banging metal on metal in the middle of the night? At first I thought it might be some kind of noise from the train tracks that were across a field and street on the backside of our home. After listening for a while, my sister and I both could hear that the sound came from the front of the house. As we lived on the third floor flat of a Victorian house, we could sit at our front window and look down onto the street. We did."

Over the next few nights, they sat together and listened to the odd noise, trying to figure out what it might be. "There was nothing to see. It was just a quiet street. No traffic, no people." Then whatever was outside the house learned of the young girls watching it. "It was sometime during the night. As we sat looking out the window, we could hear the sound travel. It came from the direction of the State Hospital and traveled down Hodges Avenue. It actually stopped what audibly seemed to be in front of our house."

For the next few minutes, the two girls sat and listened for the sound to start again. To both it seemed to be right outside their window, stopped, and although they could not see anything, it felt like something was watching them. The banging then continued and moved down the street, forcing them to run across the room and under their covers. They told their father about it the next day, but he brushed it off as some workers getting some extra time in. It would be the first of his many explanations for activity happening to his girls.

The nightwalker continued and the girls would often wake up and try to catch a glimpse of what was haunting the night.

"There was no set pattern of what days [it would] happened. It was always at night though. The next time it happened, we took our dog with us to the front window. As it had done the time before, the noise came down the street. The part that terrified us was our dog followed the sound with her head from the area of the hospital. She growled the entire time. When the noise stopped in front of our house, she growled and the hair stood up all down her back. When the banging sound resumed, she followed it with her head as it went down the street. The whole time she growled. The fact that the dog heard this and growled, to us, meant there really was something there and we didn't want to deal with it. The fact that the hair stood up on the dog's neck and back when this noise stopped in front of our house made it even more terrifying."

Valerie described the sound as metal on metal, but a heavy, steel-like metal as if someone was working late and pounding heavy beams. There was a personality to the movement she never fully realized until years later. "It felt angry, hateful, not nice. Looking back, it was kind of on a mission or something. Like it was going somewhere on purpose."

The mysterious night traveler was unsettling, but Valerie was more moved by the terrible nightmare she experienced while living in the house. One recurring nightmare might have gone unnoticed, but the nighttime disruption forced her to put more significance on it. "It was always the same. We were going somewhere and were all in the car ready to go. Then someone had forgotten something and had to go back up to the house to get whatever was forgotten but needed. I would plead and beg for whoever was going up to the flat not to go. 'Let's just go. We don't need whatever was forgotten.' Sometimes I would be the one who had to go back up and would be terrified to go. Once back up there, you couldn't come down. I remember in the dream being at the window screaming for someone to help me get down to the car. These dreams were pretty much all the same. It was always nighttime. The house was cold and windy whenever one of us had to go back up. I had these dreams for years after I left Massachusetts."

Some of the dreams were worse than others. "I would have to go into parts of the house that were very scary. I don't know why they were, but they were dream scary. I would try to get out of the scary parts and something would physically hold me back. I would try and scream for help, but no one could ever hear me."

After all of her years away, she is still unsure of how the dreams fit in, but in her mind there is a connection. "Now, I am sure someone could take these dreams apart and analyze the hell out of them and say I was afraid of the unknown or something along that line. I doubt I was ever afraid of unknown circumstances. I traveled all over the country. I hitchhiked from Lake Tahoe to Pomona by myself. I have driven up and down the California coast by myself day and night. So I am not afraid of the unknown."

To her the dreams were more than just three girls with overactive imaginations. They pointed to something disturbing in the house that all of them were feeling. They *felt* things were watching them and they were never alone. They were all too young to understand the horrors going on down the street and could not explain away what they were feeling.

Answers were hard to come by. The owner of the house lived on the first floor and was well into her eighties when the hauntings happened. Valerie remembers her as being an unfriendly lady and never felt comfortable asking her about the house. The tenants of the second floor changed often and she could never get any read on whether they had seen or heard anything. The stories stayed between the sisters, especially when their father continued to deny anything was going on. The more he denied, the more they talked amongst themselves, trapped in their own fear of the house.

The dog was not the only animal the family owned. "I had a cat while living in that flat. She was blind or had some kind of eye problem and couldn't see very well. Anyway she would sleep with me sometimes. She would feel her way to the bed and jump up at the side foot of the bed, walk up to my pillow, and crawl under the blankets. I would turn over and she would lie there and purr. One night I felt her jump up onto the bed and walk up and crawl under the covers. I turned over, only there was no cat. Nothing ever hurt me physically. I don't know if I jumped out of bed or what. This happened often for a while and then stopped."

Valerie saw the shadowy figure often described by the people of Taunton Sate Hospital in her room one night when she was in her early teens. She had gone to bed at about 8 p.m. and the night seemed normal. "I don't know if it was male, female or what, but I recall seeing it once. It stood up at the foot of my bed shortly just as I was getting into it. I dove under the covers. I was under the covers for about an hour. I remember staying there until I was drenched in sweat and my muscles ached from tension. When I did lower the covers, it was gone. I went into the living room to tell my Dad. Again he brushed it off. He told me I had been dreaming."

The answer was not good enough for her though. She knew there was something in the house, although she is unsure if he ever felt it.

"There was always a feeling of pending danger and an uneasy feel to the place. The one thing that stood out in that flat is that you always knew you were never alone. Day or night, the place was creepy."

Valerie's youngest sister, Susan, also saw the dark figure, but did not understand it until years later. While Valerie does not remember everything from the short time she was at the house, Susan spent more years experiencing odd things and seemed to be a target for whatever was in there. She was three when they moved into the house, but never felt comfortable and never felt like she was truly home.

One of the hearts of the house was the middle bedroom where the two oldest girls slept when all four of them were living there. "The front room of our house was the cold spot.

Even in Massachusetts during the summer, when it is normally hot and humid, you could find cool air in that room."

Susan's strongest memories are of the closet no one went into in the room. "We had a closet in the middle bedroom, but always kept a dresser in front of it. [It] was more like an attic door than a regular closet door." No one can remember exactly why a mirrored dresser was placed in front of it, but they remember the closet giving them the creeps. None of them ever went into the attic itself or remember any of the tenants going in there.

"Very early on the dresser was put in front of that closet. There was always a cool breeze that came from under it. I only ventured in to see what was stored in there when I was fourteen or fifteen, and was sure to do it only during the day. Even though it was summer and we had no air conditioning, I distinctly remember cool air from it. And a creepy feeling and a heavy feeling of being watched.

"The first time I ventured into it was the summer I was fourteen. I found boxes of old stuff that my parents had stored in there. I found old 78 records, which I played. I was too afraid to go in there after my dad died and left everything there. It was an odd shaped closet, weird angles, and deeper than any of the other closets, similar to the kind of storage spaces that are usually under staircases, and its door wasn't a regular door. We were on the third floor, so it probably had something to do with that. Since the actual doorway was larger than the regular closets, it had a wider door, but it wasn't a regular door. I am thinking it was formed from boards linked together somehow. Even in the daytime it felt like whatever '*it*' was, it was in there, too."

Susan thinks that whatever caused the hauntings originated in the room or the attic it led to, and used the door as a way to get into the house. This meant it walked through her room. "That room and the closet in the middle room were always the focus of '*it.*' I shared the front room with my dad. There was a period of a couple of weeks or so that my dad reminded me of when I was a teenager, and that I remembered after he told me. I would wake up just about the time he was getting into his car in the morning, which was about 3 a.m. since he was a cook and had to go in early to cook the food for the breakfast and lunch diner he worked at. During this period, I would wake up just as he was down at the car and would cry down to him to come back, that 'they' were going to get me. He would try to calm me and tell me that no one was going to get me. My mother, who slept in another room, and my sisters were there. I would tell him that they wouldn't be able to get to me in time. He remembered it more because the neighbors had complained to him about the noise of a crying three year old screaming out the window, waking everyone up."

Her father tolerated the crying, but the hauntings continued. "There was always a presence in that room, which shared a common wall with the closet from the other room. When I was about seven, I was playing a game of someone chasing me. I would run from the living room into the front bedroom, touch the foot of the bed and then act like someone was chasing me and run back into the living room. One of the times that I touched the foot of the bed, I clearly heard a voice from the front closet say, 'Who are you?' It of course scared me! Valerie even remembers that I stopped playing and just sat in the living room and didn't want to talk about it."

Susan's experiences with the presence continued even while her sisters were still in the house. In addition to the cold spots, she could sense something was there. "I was the youngest and also a brat. One night my sisters were asleep and they had a large glass jar of their Halloween candy under their bed. I was usually afraid to venture out of my room, but did this time. Unfortunately, after I was already lying under their bed, 'it' came around. I didn't see it, but could feel it. I tried lying there as still as I possibly could. It felt like it was lying next to me, staring at me. I remember the feeling of that being very strong."

And, that feeling of something being there was strongest at night. "I would be in bed and it would sometimes feel like it was standing over me, watching me. I was always way too afraid to open my eyes. I spent a lot of time learning to fall asleep breathing under the covers, afraid to move."

Not all of the hauntings were frightening. Some were just plain annoying. Susan remembers the small, day-to-day reminders that SOMETHING was there. "Since the front room was my room when I was little, there were many, many times I would be playing and some of the things I was playing with would disappear. You know you just put it down next to you and now you can't find it. Only problem is I never did find those things. I remember thinking I will find it later and wouldn't. Maybe whoever that was in the front closet took them?"

Sometimes the fear Susan felt in the house took no form. Instead it only toyed with her, making its presence known without making its presence known. "One night I woke up hungry and fixed myself some soup or something. Whatever it was, it had to be fixed on the stove. Standing at the stove, if you moved to your right just a little, it was a straight line to the front room. I was really trying to avoid it, because it was scary. That night, the presence was very strong." She continued to prepare the food, but the feelings grew.

"By the time I finished fixing whatever it was I wanted to eat, I wanted my dad. He was asleep in the living room, but I sure wasn't going to walk in the same direction of whatever that thing was, so I went around to the middle bedroom, which was now my room. I stood in the doorway from that bedroom to the living room and screamed and cried for my dad to wake up, which he didn't. And, so it went. We learned early on to just deal with feeling this invisible terror. I have to say, I saw absolutely nothing that night. But, the feeling — it was intense."

"I definitely felt threatened and afraid. It was very strange to feel all these things without seeing anything, but it was definitely coming from the front room."

Susan had moved into the room with the closet and dresser by the time she was fifteen. The room still made her uneasy, especially whatever was behind the door. One summer, right before she left, something made contact.

"The dresser faced the door to the kitchen. My bed was in the left corner, next to a window. So, if I were to wake up, I could see into the mirror, which looked into the kitchen. I could see the top half of the enamel stove. The apartment was filled with old furniture when we first moved in, and we continued to use most of the original furniture until we moved.

"One night, and I remember this clearly, I awoke to a noise. A loud noise. I wasn't sure what it was at first, but when I turned, my eyes automatically looked into the mirror. There stood something, which would have been about six feet tall. It was standing in the kitchen looking into my room, looking at me. I could see from the shoulders up over the top of the back of the stove. It looked like a combination of animals, with round eyes, horns, little animal-like ears, and a pig nose. I don't remember the rest of the face, but it was strangely round. The eyes stood out, since we made eye contact through the mirror.

"The eyes in the mirror were round and bloody looking—and they were looking directly at me. It was probably waiting for me. Its reaction to me looking at it was just to stare back at me. It was looking at me on purpose. I know that it wasn't like I surprised it or anything. It knew that I would see it when I woke up. What the screams or whatever they were meant, I don't know. It was just staring at me on purpose, but didn't come closer. Maybe it didn't have the authority to come closer? It seemed angry.

"I, of course, covered my head after that. But, it screamed a couple more times. It sounded like an animal in pain. I was wide-awake for the screams. It must have been a scream that woke me up. I stayed under the covers until I woke up the next morning."

The animal made itself known to her years later, after she had left the house. "Back in around 1982, I moved into a new apartment here in California with my two small children. My youngest was almost 2. I had a couple of dreams that were almost identical to what I was doing when awake. I was unpacking something at the counter and heard someone behind me laughing at me. I turn around and whatever I saw at 15 was sitting on my couch laughing at me. The laugh from the chair was like it was ridiculing me, mocking me. That was clear. I think that had to do with the fact that I was a Christian. I don't remember the whole dream, except that I started praying for it to leave and to leave me alone, that it had no right to be there."

The girls were never able to connect any tragedy to the house, reinforcing their belief it had some connection to the state hospital down the street. Valerie might remember more of the history of the house. It was built in the late 1800s and the original owner's daughter, elderly at the time, was the landlord when they moved in. It might have been something brought in the house from the landlord's son. According to both women, he frequented the hospital, maybe on an outpatient basis, although they are not sure why. It might have had something to do with his mother and there were whispers he was unstable because of her. While no direct evidence can link the son to anything in the house, the dark figure, and whatever walked the house, could have attached itself to him.

The force in the house might have been drawn in for another reason. Both women describe their upbringing as anything but usual. All three girls had been in foster care before moving in. Their mother was in and out of their lives, and after moving into the house she left again for the last time. The older sisters owned books on the occult, and in later years Susan was drawn to the same subject because she had found the materials they had left. She even went so far as to write something out in blood before Valerie found it and yelled at her. There was no ill intent to cause anything evil to happen and it was much more acceptable to experiment in the 1960s during the rebirth of the neo-paganism and the rise of popular Satanic cults. Regardless of their intentions, the tension and exposure to supernatural elements are both classic triggers for all types of unexplained phenomena.

The nature of the creature and the history of the area point to something older than a ghost. Spirits act in a certain way, even within the realm of the unknown. The animal-like figure seen in the mirror, its appearance years later in another location, the horrible screaming, and the influence of her dreams, point to a demon. Much like the dark figures seen in many of the towns in the Triangle and the dark men seen in Taunton State Hospital, whatever was in the kitchen fed off Susan's fear.

Later Susan came to know what was in the kitchen that night. For reasons other than her experiences in the house, Susan became a Christian in the early 1980s. It has given her strength to see how tough her childhood was, but it also gave her perspective on the happenings in her house. Once, while listening to a Christian radio station, she heard a description that matched hers. The host talked of demons, and the terror in her house made sense.

Even today her childhood has helped to mold her thoughts on the Devil. "I believe the Bible when it says that Satan and his followers are out to destroy us. What better way than to be active in someone and able to mingle around, influencing others. If you were invisible and could observe someone twenty-four hours a day, you would be well aware of everything about them, knowing their every weakness. What better way to influence temptations? What better way to know exactly how to cause them to stumble because the ultimate goal is to destroy them?"

Throughout most of the hauntings, the girls were alone, talking only to each other about what they were going through. They did not share the story with outsiders, and their father did not believe them. Before he passed away, even he was not so quick to dismiss them. "By the time I was a teenager, my dad didn't shrug the things I would say like he did my sisters," says Susan. "Maybe because we continued to say the same things? Maybe he was finally beginning to believe us? But, at this point it was just my dad and I living there." Susan is unsure if he ever experienced anything himself, but she noticed the change in his attitude, especially in the summer before he died.

After his death, all three sisters put the house behind them. They moved out of state and tried to forget the house in Taunton. It comes back though. When they think back, the time in the apartment comes back as flashes, unconnected episodes that make sense only now. Things were ignored forty years ago, passed off and hidden. The memories' only common denominators are confusion and fear, and that is what is left as the legacy of the house on Hodges Avenue.

The Other Asylum

With so many asylums in the area, it is not unusual for some of them to get lost in the shuffle. Taunton is one of the most haunted buildings in the state and Bridgewater is still running and adding to its lore. Just outside of the Triangle there are the asylums of Plymouth and the surrounding areas where reports are often confused with folklore, and sometimes just confusing. It is not unusual that Foxboro would get none of the press of its bigger brothers and sisters. Those who have experienced being there know it is not a building to be taken lightly, and the rumors are beginning to get out about the asylum time forgot. As the new trend continues, Foxboro will be reborn as condominiums, and while the protests in Danvers were loud enough to at least be acknowledged, no one is looking to Foxboro. Except, of course, for the paranormal investigators.

The hospital was originally opened in 1889 as the Hospital for Dipsomaniacs and Inebriates at Foxborough, primarily a treatment center for alcoholics and other addicts; it was the first public one in the country. It was somewhat successful in this kind of treatment, but as the other asylums in Massachusetts began filling up, they called upon Foxboro to start taking in patients well outside their normal clientele. In the early years of the twentieth century tunnels and passageways were developed to connect the isolated buildings, and the hospital began taking in mentally ill patients. The alcoholics were shipped out. All the normal problems began to spring up. The buildings became overcrowded. Then there were the reports of abuse and mistreatment. Unlike some of the other asylums in Massachusetts, there was never strong evidence of this, but the stories had enough weight to stay in people's minds.

By the time it was closed in 1975, the stories of ghosts had already started to become legend. There were screams from parts of the hospital where there were no patients and

The Foxboro State Hospital.
Courtesy of Brendan Paulson and the Abandon Photography and Urban Exploration.

doors would open and close with no one there to touch them. Shutters and blinds would open and close, usually in places where patients were incapable of moving across the room to get to them.

Trevor was employed there in the early 1970s and remembers people telling him things they had experienced. "It was a different time then. There were no ghost shows and hospitals weren't all over the TV. It was religious to the people I worked with. They used to say to ignore it because it was the Devil coming for the patients. I wasn't religious, so that didn't work for me. I know what I saw."

He was subjected to whispers and flickering lights on a nightly basis, but it was what happened near Christmas 1972 that solidified in his mind there was something after death. "This old guy was there for a long time. No family and almost comatose. One night he tells me to stop being rude and say hello to his mother. They say that's one of the signs when they know they are going to die. I felt bad and rubbed his head and told him it was going to be okay, but he was really pissed. He started to get up, and I told him to relax. He did, but kept looking in the corner of the room to a chair. It was a generic chair you still see in hospitals, but there was a slight imprint, as if someone was sitting on it.

"I left the room quickly, pretty scared there was someone in there, but came back about an hour later to check on him. The door wouldn't open. The knob turned and it wasn't locked, but I couldn't get in. It was like there was something heavy blocking it. I started to worry about the guy and jammed the door with my shoulder. It opened, and as I went into the room, I saw a dark figure jump from the chair and disappear. The guy was fast asleep." Trevor left less than a week later and never learned what happened to the man.

The real hauntings in the building began once it closed. It remained abandoned for more than twenty years, opening its doors every once in a while to host haunted houses or charity events. When the mood of the country changed and paranormal investigators and urban explorers began popping up, Foxboro became a popular place to go. It was easier to get to than some other famously haunted hospitals and was a hotbed of activity, especially for groups in the Southeastern part of the state. Their investigations and reports lifted the humble buildings to the status of Danvers and Metropolitan State in Waltham.

The reason for the hauntings is the same old story. There were reports of patient abuse and unexplained deaths. There was an obvious emotional foundation for any haunting, and the pauper graves, some still lost and unaccounted for, may be behind any number of lost souls. There is something that makes Foxboro slightly different than other abandoned asylums. The inside was still very much intact for years after it closed, although it was filthy and official documents and personal belongings were scattered and thrown about the building. Refrigerators were in their original locations, but their doors were torn off. Squatters have used the grounds, especially before the property was sold, and countless parties have been held there. There is still the feel the building was left empty at a moment's notice, as if it was left behind after a natural disaster.

Lauren lives near the old hospital and makes regular trips there as part of her paranormal investigations. She feels something is still in the building and on the grounds, and has captured what she believes are two people in windows looking down at her. Her daughter also had a negative experience at Foxboro when she accompanied her mother to the site. "My daughter, who is 16, felt like she was being chased out of the building. No one was there. She saw shadows. Wind blowing when there was no wind. It was your normal stuff that could be imagined, but it scared the beejezus out of her."

Brendan Paulson has been to Foxboro often, and the eerie feel to the place never goes away for him. He is the founder of Abandoned Photography and Urban Exploration, an organization dedicated to exploring urban buildings and documenting any paranormal activity they find. He considers the hospital one of the most haunted places in Massachusetts, and he has visited many that are in the running.

An abandoned set of stairs inside Foxboro State Hospital.
Courtesy of Brendan Paulson and the Abandon Photography and Urban Exploration.

"We want to try and get as much evidence, so we have been there a few times. We've heard people whispering or screaming in the distance. Once we started hearing footsteps—and neither of us was walking. We've heard the door slam and had the temperature drop on us." His team goes in with cameras to preserve the history people are too eager to forget, but they also bring the full paranormal toolbox with them as well, including energy meters and thermometers.

Brendan says the hospital is abandoned, but the most intimidating moments are when they encounter things that still remain active. Construction had begun on a renovation of the hospital, but there was much that still harkened back to the building's asylum days. The morgue still had tools in it, including autopsy tools. Many of the windows still had glass in them and bars on the windows. There were still beds and linen, and a few personal items scattered throughout the rooms.

Brendan thinks ghosts might stay with him after he leaves the site and somehow the emotions stick to him. "When you walk on the grounds, you start to feel sick." He has had to stop a couple times during his explorations and has reported feeling depressed and empty while on the grounds and then he suddenly felt fine afterward. It was as if he momentarily stepped into grief. His fellow investigators have reported the same thing.

The building has been known to have screams coming from it and there have been times when people in the neighborhood have reported lights on, even though at the time there was no power on in the building. There have also been bright lights seen above the building, much like a UFO or the ghost lights reported at other places throughout the Triangle. The buildings are not the only haunted places though. Nearby are two cemeteries that became the final resting place for many of the residents. The graveyards are not kept and are overgrown, with some headstones discarded in the woods and others with blood and graffiti on them. Most have the traditional number system, representing people who will never be remembered.

The cemeteries are haunted as well. Several people have reported seeing a young woman and a little girl in the area who disappear when approached. While the woman may be a former patient, there is no report of any children ever being admitted in to the hospital or dying there. The paranormal is made of the unusual though; and if the stories are more than legend, there may be an unusual reason for the ghost, such as a spirit resorting back to its younger self. Some might even say the childlike intellect of many of the patients might be mirrored in the presence of the little girl.

VinCo Properties of Boston bought the property in 2005, paying more than five million dollars for the building and its land. It began construction on residential buildings, including houses and attached condominiums, and has started removing the trash and breaking down walls. There will also be several businesses that will move onto the property. The trend to buy up these properties is well under way, and old asylums like

Danvers have progressed fairly unchallenged, but there is an odd thing happening to them. These old hospitals are suffering fires, like the one reported at Taunton. At Foxboro the arson fire happened in July of 2006 and still remains unsolved.

People say the construction trucks have moved off the property, and it would seem, at least for a brief moment, the hospital is again left behind. The trucks will return and finish the project and people will move in and start families over ground that once held the grief of disturbed minds and broken spirits. In the Bridgewater Triangle grief does not dissipate, and history, especially negative history, has a habit of coming back and touching future generations. Foxboro has always been the overshadowed asylum, even during its brief time as a paranormal attraction, so it might be used to drifting in and out of people's thoughts. For now the investigators still come, sneaking in and finding it not that hard to get in, like no one really cares if they are there in the first place.

Part Three

Stories in Stone

Triangle Cemeteries

T
he mood is set from the moment you step in. The headstones shine in the dark, giving off enough light for you to see, but never enough to read the names or break up the shadows around you. Even when you go during the day, there is a quiet that shatters your eardrums and makes your stomach twitch. You are surrounded by death, and just being there in other people's final resting place makes you feel something is not quite resting.

Cemeteries are one of the most documented locations of hauntings. Why a ghost would choose to remain in the place where its body is has never been fully explained. It might be trapped energy or confusion, but there are also too many reasons for the hauntings to not be true. In the Bridgewater Triangle, every graveyard has a story.

Riverside Cemetery

Riverside Cemetery on Main Street in Fairhaven has several hauntings attached to it. Like many ghosts of the rows, there is a story of someone hanging from the trees, victim to some tragedy in real life, and burned into some psychic plane. There have also been unexplained lights seen from the outside. Maggie had her own experience there.

"Me, my brother, and his friend were in there playing with a Ouija board and it kept coming up f-a-g. We were all giggling because we were real little and it was funny, but when we got up we noticed one of the stones near us had the initials F.A.G."

St. Stephen's Cemetery

In Attleboro, there is the infamous St. Stephen's Cemetery, one of the most rumored bone yards of the Triangle. The rumors are of a whole phantom family there; a woman, her husband, and their two-year-old daughter named Doris. Many people have reported seeing the little girl skipping in the cemetery, only to have her disappear as she turns to look at them. For some reason, Doris has been linked to this ghost, but it seems odd that a two-year-old would be big enough to skip. There are also footsteps heard on the pavement leading into the main part of the grass.

Lawrence was asked an interesting question when he was in his early thirties and had gone there looking for ghosts. "I heard singing, like that eerie little kid singing you hear in horror movies. I kept trying to follow the sound, but nothing. Then, as I was getting ready to go, a little female voice said, 'don't go. I'm lonely.' Well, it was about midnight, and I was freaked out and I ran out so fast I left a shoe there."

St. Stephen's Cemetery is also known as a haven for drug users and partiers. In between the vagrants, you might be able to find a paranormal investigator or two. A giant cross headstone for a man named Dousette has been known to glow for years. Investigators took part of it to study why, but were unable to come up with any logical reason. Even in a land known for its stones, this one was out of the reach of science. It is said they moved it to see if the glowing was a trick of light, but the headstone turned red in the night. According to the Shadowland report, a man is there to help you during your search. If you travel to the right part of the cemetery and flash your lights, he will come out of the woods and tell you the haunted tales and where to find the ghosts. This has not been confirmed and it is unclear whether the paranormal website is inferring he lives in the woods, is the caretaker, or is some spirit people have seen and talked to there.

Oak Grove Cemetery

Oak Grove Cemetery in Fall River has the grave of Lizzie Borden, the Bridgewater Triangle's most famous resident. Her plot, like everything associated with her, has become known as a place to see something unexplained. People have heard screams and cries from that part of the cemetery and two ghosts, made of nothing more than light but having form, holding hands. Some have claimed to capture Lizzie's image on film and have heard her voice in EVPs.

Knowing nothing of its haunted history, Michael and his family had an unexplained incident happen while visiting the grave. "In early July of this year we visited Lizzie Borden's house earlier in the day and then went to Oak Grove cemetery to see the Borden graves later on that evening. It was a very rainy day, but by the time we arrived at the cemetery it began to stop raining. While we were driving into the cemetery, we were listening to a Christian radio, but by the time we got to the

Borden gravesite the radio went completely static. The Borden gravesite isn't far from the front gate, but the radio went out just as soon as we reached the Borden graves. Our kids thought that was odd, but we blew it off as bad weather. After visiting the graves for a few moments my wife and I got back into the car and started to drive away. As soon as we were about fifty feet or so from the graves, [the station] came back on. My wife and I just looked at each other while the kids looked at us. And even though the Borden gravesite wasn't far away from the entrance, we couldn't find our way out, as if something was keeping us there. The front entrance was big, but we somehow got turned around and couldn't find it. We should have just backtracked, but we thought it would be easy to just go forward from the graves and find our way out. Fifteen minutes later we made it. We left Fall River as soon as we could."

The Bordens are not the only ghosts at Oak Grove. Other people have seen a man dressed in Victorian clothing and a woman dressed all in black with no face. Peter is a very concrete man who teaches high school in the area. He claims to have seen the woman while looking for the infamous Borden plot.

"She was a bit away from me but facing me. She had on a long black dress, but there was nothing where her face was supposed to be. I saw her clear and it was about noontime. She faced me and didn't move. I felt a breeze in my ear, like someone blowing, and I turned to see if there was anyone there. There was no one, but as I turned back, she was gone."

Mount Hope Cemetery

North Attleboro has its most haunted cemetery, and the rumors surrounding it have been posted on the Internet since ghost sites began to flourish at the turn of the century. Mount Hope Cemetery takes its place among the others with its dancing statue. The white statue is a replica of Jesus with his arm outstretched and pointed towards heaven. It is said if you

stare at it, the messiah will begin to move. The other legend attached to it involves Jesus leaving. On the Saturday before Easter you can go out to the cemetery and wait for the stone to disappear. It has been known to go missing between the hours of midnight and three.

Broadway Street Cemetery

"I went to see the chair. That was why the three of us would ever go to Taunton. We brought a Ouija board to see if we could talk to the little girl, and she sure had something to say."

Sam had heard the rumors of the little girl buried at the Broadway Street Cemetery for years, and was not sure if the rocking chair was real or not. He could not find it when he went, but others have said they have sat in it and seen the ghost of a little girl rocking in it. She can be seen at night as well as during the day, and others have only seen the chair move back and forth with no one on it and the wind still.

Sam and his two friends found the grave of a girl who had died young and assumed it was the child who owned the rocking chair. They set up the board and asked if anyone wanted to speak with them. "It started moving all over the place, real fast, but it was not spelling anything out. We figured maybe she couldn't spell because she was so young. We told her to move it to the left side for yes and the right for no. We asked her if she was scared and one of my friends felt arms around him, like he was being hugged, and then my other friend had her head pushed forward. We grabbed the board and ran out and I have not used it since."

Clark & Horr Cemetery

Clark & Horr Cemetery is little more than a private burial site in Lakeville that consists of two family plots. There are not many graves, but there are at least two different ghosts attached to the land there. The first is a young man, said to be in his thirties, who dances on the Clark side. The other is a formation of round red lights. There are conflicting reports, placing the number of orbs at either three or five, but they are always said to fly around in circles and then fall to the ground and fade, as if being sucked up by the soil.

Ellis Bolles Cemetery

The cemetery on Wolf Island Road is perhaps the most famously haunted site of its kind in the Bridgewater Triangle. Everyone knows about it, and at some point any talk of the paranormal in that corner eventually turns to a story someone has heard from it. It is considered an afterthought; a haunted location everyone knows about, but no one believes in. Yet one by one they tell about the urban legends associated with it, and then, just as they are about to talk about another haunting, they mention a quick little moment they had there they cannot explain.

Officially named the Ellis Bolles Cemetery, the graveyard that has been known as the place to go for a good party and for getting closer to your girlfriend for more than three centuries. People have argued, or at least misidentified, the resting area as being in Rochester, Mattapoisett, or New Bedford. Even those that go there are not sure of which town they are in.

All they know are the stories...which all begin with the hanging bodies.

Wolf Island dates back to the seventeen hundreds; many of the stones are cracked and aging, their names almost worn down from New England winters. More than two hundred years later the stories began...of the dead bodies in the trees. Residents have seen them first hand, although there have been few who want to retell the story. Most hear it as historical context and give different reasons. Most say it has something to do with the King Philip War or the Revolutionary War. It is said a colonial was living nearby and met with resistance from the enemy. A fight broke out, or a raid was conducted, and either the enemy hung him and his family or his troops fought bravely and captured their adversaries and hung them from the trees.

Other reports are of a cult that sacrificed their victims and hung them from the trees. Although there is known cult activity in the area, this does not seem too plausible.

The other reason given for the ghosts is a murder or suicide in the cemetery. Some say a man killed several people in an accident and hung himself near their graves in his guilt. This fits in with some of the car legends told about the cemetery, but has never been confirmed. Another tells of two people getting close in the car when something happens to force the man out. The woman stays and begins to hear a scraping on the door or the roof of the car. The man is found dead the next morning, either with his hand on the door trying to get in, or hanging from a tree above the roof, his feet just touching. This is the least likely story as it is a well-known myth that has been proven false over the years.

The best candidate for the haunting, if there actually is one, is the war story. Regardless of the origin, people have seen dark figures hanging from the trees. Sometimes it is only one person, but often they see at least half a dozen bodies swaying from branches.

Tom claims to have a picture of the hangings, although the shot was taken at night and there is little that can be made out at all. He holds onto it as he tells his story, and to listen to him, the picture is not the only evidence they were there.

"I know this sounds weird, but the night I took the picture I could see them with my eyes. That's why I took it. We were playing around, waiting for the Mustang, when I heard a low moan. I looked up, and saw at least five people hanging from the trees above me. I shouted to the guys I was with, but none of them saw anything. I'm more sensitive, but at least they heard the moan."

There are other strange, unexplained visitors to the burial grounds. Luanne, paranormal investigator, received an interesting EVP (electronic voice phenomena) when she visited the cemetery. While asking questions near the grave of a man with Freemason markings on his headstone, she received a faint voice that said, "Freemason."

A woodsman with an axe has also been seen in and around the graveyard. He is said to be very intent on what he is doing, walking with purpose, and not paying attention to the modern world. People have seen this ghost for the past thirty years, and some of the accidents that have taken place nearby are attributed to swerving to avoid hitting him. He is a tall man, well over six feet, which is roughly the height of another figure seen in the cemetery. This one appears as only a fog or a dark, solid shadow. It is hard to tell if the spirit is the same, but both have been known to come up quickly on parked cars or chase them if they drive by too slowly.

Another urban legend has a home there. The timeless "Bloody Mary" story is attached to the cemetery as well. People were told to go to the back wall and touch it while saying the name "Mary" five times. Karen remembers the stories from her youth in the 1980s. "The road is paved now, but we used to go out there and call for Mary. It never worked, but we were all freaked out."

There is also another tale of a glowing headstone. No one who remembers the story can recall the woman's name, and over time she has just been called Mary as well. In the pitch darkness of the road, which until recently had no streetlights, one grave would glow an eerie green in the night. This is a fairly common cemetery legend, but there is a Triangle twist to it. People say that if you drive nearby and angle your car when you see it, a woman will appear and the headstone will "turn off." The woman is said to be in a white nightgown and will appear for only a few seconds. People who tried it in the 1980s and 1990s report never seeing the woman, but having a white orb rise from the ground.

The most famous stories at Wolf Road revolve around the car. It is said to be a white Mustang, but the story itself dates back before Mustangs were produced. Someone died near the road in the car and his ghost, and the spectral manifestation of his prized possession, are said to remain there. The car will appear in the rearview mirror of anyone stopping to look at the cemetery at night. Much like the Mad Trucker, he will honk his horn and flash his lights before fading into thin air.

This ghost is more active than other car spirits who cruise through town legends. This one has been known to force cars off the road and has been seen replaying the accident over and over again. It is said if you park and see the accident, you will have one yourself on the way home, although no one has ever been able to confirm having seen it and crashing or knowing anyone who has. There has been one confirmed accident where someone parking with his girlfriend saw headlights and then heard the crash of a car. Not knowing the legend but not wanting to get caught hanging out, he took off and hit a nearby tree because he was distracted and moving too fast. When the police came, his car was totaled, but the other car was never found. This might be the origin of the tree aspect of the legend and the accident warning.

The stories change so often, and the legends are so diverse, you have to wonder if the haunting tells more about the living than the dead. Luanne heard about the stories long before she started investigating the paranormal. "There is supposedly an accident that happened before I was born. You had to go down to Wolf Island Road to this particular corner where he drove off the road into a tree. You shut your car down and flash your lights three times and off in the distance you'll see headlights flash at you three times. This mustang comes flying up the dirt road and goes through your car. If you get out and look at your roof, you'll have tire tracks going over your roof."

Some legends are best when mixed.

Remembering the Dead

S ome places in Massachusetts are marked by the tragedies that befall them. Their histories are set off by years of calamity and residents of the places learn their town genealogy by the stories they hear of lives lost. Danvers, Massachusetts, for example, has seen the Salem Witch Trials and the birth of Danvers State Hospital, and in recent years, explosions and fires that have rocked the town. Few lives have been lost, but there is just enough to make people know that not all is right in the town.

The Bridgewater Triangle invites these timelines. Towns like Freetown and Newport alternate between the criminal and the supernatural, but one of the most marked towns might be Brockton. The City of Champions has given rise to Santa Claus, the baseball glove, and Rocky Marciano and Marvin Hagler. Their football team was once the template for all New England Friday Nighters, but the town has drawn something darker in. While the current city is known for its crime rate, most of it is related to gang activity and common crime...but there is an uncommon criminal element to the city as well, and every once in a while it boils to the top and shows itself again.

Then there are the disasters. In 1949, the Strand Theatre Fire took the lives of thirteen firefighters. The memory is still very much alive in the town, with memorials being built and charities still raising money for those left behind. Before that, there was the R. B. Grover & Company Shoe Factory Boiler Explosion.

On the morning of March 20, 1905 hundreds of employees had their day shattered when the boiler in the building exploded, sending the machine through the roof and causing an intense fire fueled by escaping gas. Fifty-eight people were killed and 150 were injured, some of which were never identified.

Thirty-six of those unidentified made their way to a common grave inside Melrose Cemetery in Brockton. The town later built a memorial to those souls, but there might be something restless in the cemetery that needs something more. For years people had reported hearing laughing in parts of it, but then other visitors – those detached from the paranormal world – began to experience something profound. At least that is what people who have seen a vanishing man who rests near the monument feel.

William is one of those men who have seen the ghost of a middle-aged man who seems transfixed by the grave. In January of 2006 he visited the grave of his grandfather who had passed away years earlier. "It was his anniversary, and every year I go there and talk to him. It's been a long time. I was just a kid when he died, but I always felt connected to him. Same routine every time. I get a large coffee and drink it while I talk to him."

William noticed something unusual on this visit. "There was a guy near the Boiler memorial. I noticed him because we were the only ones in the cemetery and he was in a white shirt. It was pretty cold, and this guy was standing there in nothing but a shirt." William says the man was not shivering nor did he seem to notice the weather at all. He was about twenty feet away, and there was no breath coming from his mouth.

"I turned to tell my grandfather I thought this guy was crazy, and when I turned around, I mean it was only two seconds later, he was gone." He thought it was odd, and having never paid any mind to the stone, moved over to see what it was. As he got closer, he noticed there were no tracks in the new snow, including where the man had been standing. The ground was totally undisturbed around the grave.

"That's when I knew it had been a ghost. I always thought it had to be night or something. In movies, the whole thing is scary, but I didn't get scared until I got closer. I didn't even believe in ghosts, and I'm still not a hundred percent sure. I just know what I saw. It was like he had been there, but there was no proof. He had just vanished and there was nothing left behind."

William was unsettled when he learned more about the explosion, and decided to remember it his own way. In January of 2007 he brought two cups of coffee to Melrose and had two conversations.

He describes the man as being a bit older than thirty and a bit under six feet tall. He was wearing brown pants and a white, shirtsleeve shirt, like an undershirt. The man's brown hair was cut short, and although he never saw his face because he was turned away, he said his skin was pale. He witnessed the whole thing on a cold but clear day, and the figure appeared solid and of this earth when he first saw it.

Later that year, around Halloween, he and some friends were watching a television show about ghosts when he decided to tell what had happened to him at the cemetery. A few of the people he was with said they had gone into the graveyard at night when they were in high school and had seen red and white lights floating near the common grave for the victims and had run out.

Amy had experienced something a bit more. "When Will told me what happened, I knew it was the same guy. Right down to the shirt, it was the same man I saw. I didn't tell him right away, but it really disturbed me when I saw him."

Amy had been visiting her aunt and leaving flowers in May of 2006. She saw a man standing in front of the memorial, reaching out and running his hand over the names, like he was trying to read them. "Maybe that's just the idea I got knowing what it was, but now I think he was looking for his name on the memorial.

"I watched him for a few seconds, thinking it was strange he was touching it. He was young. I thought maybe he was looking for his great-grandfather or something. Then he stepped away and got very angry. His hands went to his side and he made fists. I was about forty feet away, so I got a pretty good look at him. All I remember is he had this strong chin, like a movie star. He looked right at me and his mouth started to move. I didn't hear anything, but I knew he was trying to talk to me. Then, right as I watched, he faded away. His mouth was still moving, but he just disappeared."

Amy felt from the moment she saw him she was looking at a ghost. She describes it like a feeling in her stomach that told her she was seeing something she shouldn't be. She also describes the noise stopping in the cemetery and everything seeming to move in slow motion.

"I looked at him for almost thirty seconds. It wasn't out the corner of my eye or anything. He was a ghost, and he was so sad and angry. It has to be one of those men who died. He's trapped here and maybe doesn't understand what happened to him. At that moment I was sad for him, but when I think about it now, I'm scared. I have always believed in spirits, but now I know. They could be watching me when I don't want them to."

There have been no public reports of the young man before 2006, so it is a mystery as to why two friends, on separate days, saw him. Perhaps there is something about the one-hundred-year anniversary that set off energy or forced a restless soul to come back and try and solve its own death a hundred years later. The reason for the haunting is as baffling as the ghost itself.

Today those who died are still remembered, and the accident helped to reform boiler safety for the whole country. That would seem to offer little consolation for the man William and Amy saw at Melrose Cemetery. For him remembering is not enough. After more than a century, the lonely man in Brockton wants to understand.

The Cemeteries at the Apex

Palmer River

I t is right for one of the corners of the Bridgewater Triangle to experience more paranormal activity than most towns within, and the foundation of the activity there begins with its haunted resting places. The town of Rehoboth feels at times to have more cemeteries than houses, and more ghosts than the horse it has become known for. Most are small plots of land, covered with a few stones and overgrown with grass. Others are testaments to the history of the town and stick out as places of beauty. People travel to explore and to make rubbings, but they become very different places at night. The sun sets and the stories start—an entire book could be dedicated to nothing more than the rows of Rehoboth.

Of the dozens of cemeteries there, none are more written about and talked about than the Palmer River burial ground and the Old Village Cemetery. They might be the most famous, and the most haunted, in the area. There are more famous people buried in Boston and Salem that have the history, but in Rehoboth...

The ghosts come out, and the energy runs down the winding roads, connecting these unrelated resting places.

Too often people associate a haunting with an ancient Indian burial ground, but perhaps the most haunted place is the bone yard you can still see with your own two eyes.

Palmer River Burial Ground

The Palmer River Burial Ground, originally called the Ye Olde Palmer's River Burial Ground, has been around longer than many of the states in the western part of the country. It gets its name from the river flowing nearby and from its relation to the church in front of it. The official name is the Lake Street Cemetery, but no one calls it that much. The burial ground name lends itself to something older, something unexplained and foreign that suits the land well. No one has been buried there for more than a century, but the grounds are not forgotten. People still go there, and their reasons for visiting help to define the name for them. The Lake Street Cemetery is where people are buried that can be appreciated for its picture of a time gone by. The Palmer River Burial Ground is haunted.

People have reported seeing things there for more than three decades, even before the recent development nearby, and before it was brought to the public by Charles Robinson. He said that there have been sightings of a small boy who was "grotesque" and had a habit of staring and vanishing. This story is not something out of the past. The little boy is still being seen, at times by people who have never read Robinson's articles and books.

Kristy loved to visit cemeteries. As a teenager in Middleboro, she would sneak out at night and write poetry and smoke cigarettes while sitting on top of tombstones. "I wasn't a Gothic person or anything. It had nothing to do with wanting to see ghosts or vampires or anything. My house was pretty hectic, and it was the only way to clear my mind. When I grew up, I just kept doing it. I do it during the day now, but it has the same affect on me. I'm chill." When she heard about the number of cemeteries in Rehoboth, she knew she had to try it out.

"All that time in all those cemeteries, and I never had a single ghost show itself. Hell, I didn't even believe in them. I liked a good scary story, but never thought I would see one. Until Palmer. I had just entered and was reading the dates on the stones. I was thinking about how old they were, and a voice inside my head said, 'We're not all old.' I knew it didn't come from me."

The feeling was different than in any of the other cemeteries she had been in before, and for the first time she felt uncomfortable in one. She walked back to the entrance slowly, looking around for what might be talking to her. "Then I saw a little kid. I assumed it was a boy, but he kind of had long hair, blond, and I didn't get a good look at him. He ducked behind a headstone a ways away from me and laughed. I called out to him, but he wasn't there. I walked behind the stone, but there was nothing there."

Bree considered the cemetery her own private paranormal training ground for a time. Once she received her first piece of evidence from it, she continued to go back, trying to get the most accurate proof she could. For a while it became an obsession for her, and her trips there always gave her just enough to continue her search of the unknown.

In May of 2004 she made her first trip to Palmer River. She took along a camera and snapped pictures before her camera mysteriously died on her. When she developed the pictures later, one had a smear of light on one of the headstones. "That caught my eye. It was really strange. I kept going back. I wanted to see if I could catch it on two different mediums. There's something there. I don't know what it is, but it's definitely there."

She began carrying a digital recorder and a digital camera whenever she went, trying to capture something that would explain what was going on there. She also began taking her father along because he was becoming increasingly interested in ghosts the more she went. On one trip they separated as he went back to the car and she tried to record EVPs. Everything seemed normal until she met him at the car. "The first thing he asked me was, 'Were you scared?' I said, 'No, why?' He said he had heard me scream. It wasn't me. It freaked me out because he said it was my voice. I was recording the whole thing and we were pretty close to each other. It was not on the audio recorder." When she looked at the pictures she had taken when she got home, there was an unexplained halo of light surrounding the headstone of a woman named Rebecca Smith. The more she goes there, the more anomalies she finds on her pictures.

Another time she went to Palmer, Bree got home to find she had gotten voices on her tape recorder. She was walking through the cemetery and was wondering out loud whether the little boy who has been reportedly seen there has a headstone. At that precise moment on the tape, she heard a woman's voice crying. "It was just so perfectly weird. I didn't hear anything when I was saying it. It was a conversation with myself." Another time she went she got a deep, low male voice saying, "People shouldn't be here." The evidence she was getting inspired her to keep at it, and going to Palmer became a weekly thing. The trips only ended when her interest in the paranormal began causing activity in her house, forcing her to stop.

Laura had no intentions of even starting. She had no interest in the paranormal and no desire to have something follow her home. Instead, she had a love of history and visited the cemetery for the challenge. "I read this story about a guy in Canada who was going to old cemeteries and researching people and then putting their history on the headstone for people to see. I thought that was cool and wanted to do the same thing."

She traveled through two towns to get to Palmer, but was delighted when she saw the state of the graves and the classic New England feel of the land. She began walking the rows looking for a good candidate. "Everything went into slow motion. I don't mean it felt like forever, I mean it literally went into slow motion. Leaves were blowing and they blew in slow motion. I saw a young man, maybe about twenty, dressed in old army clothes. He walked in front of me and touched each headstone as he went. When he reached the last one, he dissolved. Then things got normal speed again."

It is unclear exactly what Laura experienced. She was frightened enough to never return to the cemetery to see what it was like on a normal day, and she did not get a good look at the man she saw because she viewed him from behind the whole time. She has looked at different pictures to see if she could identify the uniform in history books, but she has been unable to find it. After the fact, she felt it might not have even been American because she did not remember seeing a flag. The man could have been someone laid to rest there, but she might have also experienced a residual haunting of someone who visited the graveyard for some reason, perhaps in respect of old army buddies, and his grief was strong enough to leave an impression. The sighting might also have been some kind of astral projection.

Old Village Cemetery

Like many things about Ye Olde Palmer, that secret never leaves the cemetery.

The Old Village Cemetery might not be as romantic as Palmer, but the activity is much more consistent and the stories from there come easier and quicker. The ghosts there are notorious, and according to people who have seen and heard things, not all who are dead are happy about it. In addition to the ghosts, there is something unnatural about the woods surrounding the cemetery. People have seen and heard things—they feel like the woods are alive somehow, living and breathing and watching them.

The stories of the cemetery begin much more harmless than that. Dozens of people have heard an offensive cat call while visiting. The noise has been heard not only by paranormal investigators who have visited, but also from mourners who travel there to lay flowers on relatives' graves. There are people who have never heard of the hauntings there, but who share their stories once they hear other people talking.

Jody heard it while she was there talking to her grandmother. "Just talking quietly. I usually just sit with her and tell her how things are going. Then I heard this whistle, like a construction worker or something. It was so loud I thought it was right behind me. I looked, but there was no one there. I thought it was inappropriate until I heard there is a guy that whistles there. I still go there to see her, but I hope I don't hear it again."

Luanne is a paranormal investigator from the area who has spent time in most of the haunted locations known in the Triangle. She has been to the Old Village Cemetery several times, and knows there is something there.

"You just get a feeling about a place. That place has it."

Old Village Cemetery.

One of the first times she went she walked around getting a feel for the location. She heard a low, male voice, barely audible, like a whisper. The voice followed her and her partner the entire time, until she finally was able to hear it clearly say, "hello," to her. She snapped a picture right at that moment and had a "soft" human figure in the corner of the shot. Luanne made several audio recordings while she was there. On one she heard a male voice talking over her while she dictated what they were doing. Although she cannot make out what the man is saying, his tone is somewhat angry and threatening.

The man might be a ghost that has been seen and documented by Robinson and several other paranormal investigators over the years. He is an old man who has threatened people on occasion and has a tendency to yell, swear, and attack an invisible foe. He is a phantom who has all the characteristics of a residual haunting. He is most known for kneeling in one part of the graveyard and praying before a headstone. He then falls into a hysterical depression and cries, followed by maniacal laughter. He does not see the people watching him, or at least he does not care about them. He has also been known to get very angry and attack someone who witnesses cannot see. He appears to knock whomever it is down and then proceeds to kick him while he is on the ground. In addition to those stories and accounts in *The New England Ghost Files*, the old man has made himself known to people since then.

"I was in there for fun. Trying to scare my friends. Right. I'm the one with the nightmares now." David was a teenager when he first went to Old Village. They were planning on having a few drinks and had just opened his first can when he leaned against a headstone. "I'm not even kidding. A voice told me to get off of him. There was no one there and I hadn't even sipped yet. It scared us, so we ran. We even left the beer. So when Halloween rolled around, we wanted to go back to get scared."

According to David, they arrived around midnight and after looking for the headstone that had yelled at him, they decided to get a Ouija board and use it. "We started asking questions and the little thing was flying around. It was almost moving without us touching it. It made no sense what it was saying. Then we heard this low moan and looked. There was this figure, like a man, walking back and forth. He was walking, but I couldn't hear what he was saying. Angry though. We thought he was some old drunk, but he saw us and started walking towards us."

Although they were three strong teenagers, they began to back away as he got closer. Then, says David, he turned around and ran back to where he had come from, and as he did, he became transparent and could no longer be seen.

"We were freaked. We basically ran out, but we heard him call to us. The faster we ran, the louder he got. I didn't exhale until I got home."

David's experience points to a more complex spirit in the cemetery. If the two men are the same, he appears to be two different kinds of ghost. At times he acts very much like a residual, unthinking ghost, but he has also been known to address people and even chase them, implying there is also intelligence there. There may be another explanation for the ghost's behavior. He might be an intelligent ghost who replays his own past and gets caught in a negative energy loop of his own life, with his spirit somehow trapped in the cemetery to relive an event that happened someplace else. This indicates a very complex afterlife, which is the appeal of the paranormal investigator.

Bree had her encounter with the man, or a spirit she thinks is the man, while she was still actively visiting cemeteries. She had heard about it, and decided it would be an excellent place to try and get the ultimate evidence she was in search of. The first time she was there, the setting was something out of a ghost story; so much so, she hesitates to tell the story. "It was something so obvious you would think, 'Wow, that's a cliché horror story.' But it happened."

Soon after entering, she and her group were immersed in an unnatural fog that followed them as they walked through. The temperature dropped severely. A cop was making a pass just outside the graveyard, and they tried to get his attention in an attempt to talk to him before he noticed them and asked what they were doing there. For some reason they were drawn to the woods on the outskirts of what has been the active burial area. This part of the woods has been known to draw people in with short flashes of light and floating orbs, much like the Pukwudgie reports in other areas of the Triangle. People feel watched, and lighthearted investigators strolling through the grounds stopping there will notice a change of energy.

Bree felt it that night. "There was something evil there. I couldn't see it, but it was there." They walked deeper into the woods, unsure of what was drawing them in. "We were at the point when the woods were getting thick and there was a mist in that section." According to Bree, it came out of nowhere, and when they decided to turn around and head back, it followed them.

The night was not quite over for them. As they moved back towards the gates to leave, they heard the cat call that so many people had talked about before. One of the people she was with whistled back. "Just as we were going, something whistled back

Another haunted area of the Old Village Cemetery.

again and then one more time." While the whistles and the fog might not be solid proof of anything more than practical jokes and overactive imaginations, when Bree took a closer look at her photos when she got home, there were faces in several of the shots. The photos in the woods show a grayish figure hovering close to the group.

Most experiences in the cemetery are nothing more than brief glimpses, and the aura of the haunting is based more

on the amount of stories and not so much on the intensity of a single one. Many people have reported seeing the man in the cemetery, but he is not the only ghost who has been spotted there. Several people have reported seeing orbs of light, especially in the northern area of the graveyard. There is also a woman who glows white and floats a few feet above the ground. These reports are mostly second-hand stories and might be more legend than a real haunting.

Then there is Alice. She was in the cemetery with her friend and her friend's dog. "We were reading the headstones and her dog started to purr, like when he gets petted. His head was up and his nose was twitching, so my friend thought there was a bug near him. She tried to shoo away what might be there, and he hit the ground. Then we saw what looked like a misty figure, then behind it a reddish circle. We got scared and left, but the dog stayed. He was on all fours and looking straight ahead, and his nose was still twitching. He went back and he didn't move. Then we heard a little girl, or what sounded like a little girl, laugh at us."

Alice seemed to encounter another one of the more famous ghosts at the Village. According to Robinson and other witnesses, a little boy also makes his home there. He glides through the rows in a playful manner and moved without his feet touching the ground. Other people say he bounces or hops, almost like he is skipping through a field and not a graveyard. He laughs when people try to catch him, and appears and disappears in different places like he is playing 'catch me if you can.' Most who come across him feel there is nothing playful about him, but something sinister they cannot fully explain.

This was not the impression Alice was left with. She met the boy as she was walking by the cemetery one day. "It was about two in the afternoon and pretty hot. All of a sudden I felt this cold breeze brush by my arm. There were leaves blowing, but there was no wind. I switched places with my friend as we walked by, but she felt something brush by her too. We started to walk faster because we wanted to get out of there, but then we heard him. A little boy's voice said, 'No, don't go. I'm having fun.' We turned around and I swear we saw the face of a seven or eight year old pale boy for at least five seconds. Then he disappeared." She has never seen him again, but was not scared after he spoke. She felt sorry for him.

It is hard to say what may still be partly alive in the cemeteries of Rehoboth. They have had centuries to collect personalities and to collect stories. The two are connected in the small town where local legend is the foundation of so much of the culture. Each one has its own story, and people talk of the ghost there without sarcasm in their voice or an ulterior motive. That might be part of the problem. Too many times the stories begin with, "It's that cemetery, or was it the other one?" Stories get muddled over time and the two most notorious cemeteries, Palmer River and Old Village, collect them like scrapbooks of all the local hauntings.

Part Four

A
Triangle
Within the Triangle

The Robinson Hauntings

The Haunted Hornbine School in Rehoboth.

Anyone looking to get started in paranormal investigating needs to look no further than Rehoboth. The town is out of the way and looks like the set of a small town ghost movie. The modern world is there, but it is reserved for the main roads of the town. Drive off of Route 44, and you would expect to see a horse and buggy just as much as a car. That is not too far from the truth. The town is known for its horse breeding and training farms. The land is steeped in history and is well connected to what the past means to the people who live there now. When Loren Coleman first set out his lines of the odd, Rehoboth must have seemed like a natural ending point. There are few towns in New England that can boast as many haunted places in such a small area, and there are very few who offer an investigator a night out with the guarantee something is going to happen. Since Coleman's book was first released, the true nature of Rehoboth has come to light, and some of the history hides itself from the history books.

It was Robinson's book, *The New England Ghost Files*, that opened the eyes of New Englanders to the number of spirits that make their home in the town. As a resident of Rehoboth, the research was right in front of him, and using first-hand accounts and known legends, he created the scene for those that followed. There are few who like a good ghost story in Southeastern Massachusetts that do not have the book or have not read it. The asking price for the out-of-print book ranges from thirty to seventy dollars online, and multiple websites steal information from it to fill their pages with stories. The publisher of the book has since gone under, but a reprint has been in the works for years. That rumor might be as much a myth as anything in the Triangle.

The hauntings in Rehoboth have two lives; the first is the hauntings there before 1994, which was the year the book was published. Stories were swapped, and people saw and heard ghosts un-influenced by anyone else's stories. The ghosts became a town phenomenon, and details shifted in the retellings. Then came the book and the mania it gave birth to. After its publication, the stories continued, but also changed. While some are the making of investigators looking to find what Robinson told of, others are the tales of those who had the courage to come forth only after others had told their stories. Many of them are nothing more than legend...ghosts stories that occur in most towns across the country and become transplanted to Massachusetts's most haunted address.

The Hornbine School

The little one-room schoolhouse on Hornbine Road is a representation of the town's commitment to the past. The school originally opened in 1845 and was one of more than a half dozen schools used to service the town. It educated both male and female students up to "high school" until it was closed in 1937. It was restored and reopened to the public in 1968, but it now educates in a different way. As one of the town's many historical landmarks, it has become a field trip destination and a tourist attraction for people traveling through that part of the state.

People have had experiences there for more than twenty years, and many have tried to find rational explanations for the giggling they hear. Robinson wrote in his book of a schoolteacher who visited the town. She glanced through a window to see a teacher and class hard at work inside. She waited to speak to the fellow educator, but no one ever came out. Even though there was no way to leave the school without being seen, the entire class – teacher and all – had disappeared.

Other experiences have not been nearly as dramatic. Becky loved to go to the school because she had a thing for history. She lived a few towns over, but for her it was a special place. "I know it sounds corny, but I liked it. I'd drive the twenty minutes every other week to go there. Just to see it and hang out there." She feels there is a reason for the connection. "Maybe I was a student there in another life. It feels like that. I can't imagine wanting to go back to school once you've passed on, but I still think I went there."

In 1997 Becky says she went there right before dusk. Like always, she parked her car a ways away and walked to the school. She liked to approach the building, almost as if she was on her way to school. "I saw a dark figure walk through the door. It wasn't like it was scary. It was more like it just was a shadow of a person." She continued to walk and found the door locked and the building empty. "It should be haunted. It's a great little place."

Others have heard laughing on the side lawn of the school. While on the grass, they hear a giggle, but cannot find anyone in the area. The noise has been known to jump around the yard, and often times other voices join in.

The Old Ruins of the Shade Factory

In 1884 the mill on Shade Pond burned down. It was not the first fire there, and it was not the first in a line of misfortunes to befall the place. The fire was, many think, the trigger for a haunting that continues to this day...long after the final piece of cotton ran through.

Originally established as the Palmer River Manufacturing Company by the people of Rehoboth, the mill opened in 1810 on the site of another failed company. It had little success producing cotton yarn until it expanded to include fine cotton cloth, which was in much more ready need for the people of the time. It burnt down in 1831 and had moderate success until the Civil War limited the amount of cotton the company could take in and convert. The final fire of 1884 would mark the end of the cotton and an end to business on the site all together. The foundation is about all that remains now, barely noticeable among the tall grass. What remains is a little stone, a bit of history, and a few ghost stories passed on by residents and paranormal investigators.

Again, *The New England Ghost Files* became the source of information for people looking to find ghosts within the Triangle. In the book, Robinson tells of a couple who often walked in the area near dusk. On four separate occasions they came across an unexplained apparition on the site of the old mill while on the other side of the pond. The first encounter was with an older man standing at the ruins in old-fashioned clothes. He disappeared after they called to him, but the next night he was there again, and this time he was looking directly at them. He again disappeared, but when the woman went back by herself a week later, he was back. This time, however, the man vanished and then reappeared a few feet behind her. She ran away in fear, but the same situation played itself out almost a year later, only this time she didn't run. The man walked away from her and slowly began to fade into nothing.

Unlike other haunted areas, the source of the ghost is hard to trace. While the fires in the mill were both rumored to be arson, no one died in them. This makes the old man a mystery, but also leaves another haunting at the site as a complete enigma. People hear cries, most usually at dusk, from the place where the business once stood. The noise is like someone in pain. One man heard the screams and ran to the source. From the same side of the bank, he saw a complete building engulfed in flames. He claims the fire emanated no heat, and gave off no smoke. It was as if he was watching a replay of the fire. As he turned to get the attention of his friend, the entire scene disappeared.

Another man saw someone come out of nowhere and hit the water. He was on the other side of the pond when he heard a man yelp. He followed the noise with his eyes and was amazed to see a man in mid-air, as if he had just jumped from the window of a building that did not exist anymore. The ghost vanished when he hit the water without a splash.

While these stories display the dramatic nature of the haunting, it is the day-to-day stories that remain in the air for the residents. While the pond is a peaceful place for those who go there, the foundation has a heavier air to it. Some feel unnerved or uncomfortable being there, a stark contrast to the welcome walk that led them there. Many have reported feeling watched. The most unsettling aspect of their experience is the suddenness of the feeling. They are fine as they walk to the stone, and often feel fine eight out of ten times. Then, without any reason or pattern, the place feels different. People often dismiss how someone feels in a place, especially in the days of digital camera evidence and EVPs, but for the people who have experienced the sensation, it is as convincing as a picture or a recording.

While the site itself might make people feel like they are not alone, the people who actually see something are usually in a different location on the pond. A group of investigators went there in 1998 in an attempt to document the Rehoboth hauntings. While across the river, waiting to spot the old man, one investigator was pushed and another felt her legs being grabbed by an unseen hand. In 2007, Haunted Paranormal, an investigative group out of Rhode Island, was doing a location report for the radio show "Spooky Southcoast" and its members experienced the exact same thing.

Whatever might be at the old factory was born from sorrow. The man spotted at the site was lonely and sad, a feeling many get when they enter the site. Was someone hidden at the site when one of the fires broke out, or is it guilt left over from another time? It might have something to do with the repetitive nature of the work. A ghost might just be use to clocking in and staying. There are no records giving the reason for the original sawmill closing, and most locals feel it was just that the well had dried up for it. Rehoboth has historical cemeteries, but many of its dead lie unmarked. The town is known as a site for Native American burial sites. Perhaps the location, close to the water, provided a peaceful resting place the same way it now offers sanctuary to the townspeople who go there as the sun sets. The land itself might hold some part of the secret. No business on the spot has ever been able to be successful.

The House on Providence Street

There are many stories that spark interest in the paranormal. They say requests for exorcisms went through the roof in the 1970s after the release of the "Exorcist," and paranormal activity increased after the premiere of "Ghost Hunters." For Rehoboth, no single story may have sparked more haunted tales and more people to hit the road trying to capture ghostly evidence for themselves than an article that appeared in the *Rehoboth Reporter* featuring a haunted house on Providence Street. As people tell about their adventures looking for ghosts, many credit the story by Charles Robinson for inspiring them to get out and find local haunted areas.

People in town had already known of the house before it appeared in the fall of 2003. It was one of those places in the neighborhood everyone said was haunted and the lore was enough to keep some people away while drawing others in. The house was an old farmhouse with a cornfield and the rumor was that an elderly woman who lived in a nursing home in Rhode Island owned it. It was reported to have a view of the Palmer River and might have been built on Native American burial land, although there is little proof of this and the Indian cemetery has been used as the default reason for any unexplained haunting in the Triangle.

Neighbors avoided the house, but spoke openly about what they saw. They reported seeing faces in the window, especially on the third floor of the house. The ghost was that of a young, black haired woman who would appear in one window, then evaporate in smoke and appear in another window in the house. There were lights that would turn on and off, even though no one had lived there for years. Neighbors walking by would also hear a woman laughing, describing her as both very young and elderly. A mist was seen in the yard and field that would float on clear days and move like a person.

The most disturbing haunting seemed to be associated with an old piano left on the first floor. There would often be piano music wafting from the open windows late at night. The windows were usually closed, but when the music broke the silence of the evening, an invisible hand would also open the house up so everyone could hear. An old woman had been seen near the instrument, and she was always said to be naked and is sometimes rocking back and forth and laughing.

Alex had read the story, but he had walked by the house for years before. He had always been into ghosts, and the house was a perfect place to try and get a picture of something unusual. "My friend and I went in to just get some pictures. Ghosts exist, I'm sure of that, but we didn't think anything would happen. I thought after the story came out, I figured they'd tear the place down, so I wanted to say I was there.

"We basically tried to spend the night. Not likely. Whatever was there knew we were up to no good and wanted us out."

Alex was systematically going through the rooms taking pictures and noticed the famous fog outside. He snapped a few shots and went downstairs to tell his friend. As he told his story, he heard footsteps from where he had just been.

"I stood there and listened as the floor creaked like someone was walking to us. Down the hall and then to the stairs. I saw a dark shadow run across the top of the stairs, and then heard the stairs creak as the ghost walked down towards us. I ran out of there without my camera and I think I was screaming. Big tough guy I am."

Another person reported her friends had gone in looking for the ghosts. "They said there were all old appliances left and old time curtains in the windows. Kids trashed it and the usual satanic crap was sprayed all around and there had been fires in the house. It's a shame. It could have been a nice place."

The description echoes Manny's experience. He had gone in after hearing of the article in the *Reporter* and left almost at once. "Like an amusement park, we were going in and another group was running out. All they said was, 'Good luck,' as they ran by us. The place was a mess, and we walked through the rubble looking for a souvenir. I felt something touch my leg and then tap my shoulder, and I was out of there."

A police officer from Dighton took his seven-year-old son to the house to squash his interest in ghosts. There was nothing to them, and he would prove it. He parked in front and turned off the engine. Almost at once, hands came up from the ground and tried to stop them from getting out, making him turn the engine back on and drive as fast as he could back to his own town.

Bree spoke to the officer who encouraged her to check for herself. She and her friends went and found the house much as everyone else had. "We were going to go up and take some pictures, but we got an eerie vibe. We snapped a few from the outside, but the camera disappeared. We tore that car apart and never found it."

A few weeks later someone burned the house down to the ground. It was not the first time a fire had struck the house, but this one proved to be the fatal blow. The haunted house on Providence Street is no more, and with it dies the evidence of one of the strongest hauntings from one of the most haunted towns in Massachusetts. The myth continues to grow, and as more people come forward, the more the town learns to embrace the house it once cringed from.

Loren Coleman's apexes and definition of the Bridgewater Triangle can be challenged and scrutinized. Why are some towns, with almost no activity, included and others that lie a few miles outside not.

One thing that cannot be challenged is Rehoboth's claim as a true haunted hotspot, and in the scope of paranormal investigating and legend hunting, it is like the grail.

Some of the stories are majestic, stretching out across decades and touching different generations. Others are new and seen through the eyes of the modern ghost hunter. Three hauntings in Rehoboth just touch the surface of the activity there, and as you continue to scratch, you may learn the only way to get out again is to leave town.

Massachusetts'
Most Famous Ghost

People from New England survive on a history of oral tradition passed down by word of mouth in accents that sound funny to the rest of country. Whether it is the sports they play or the lives they live, the people are natural storytellers. Many things that happen within the Triangle become the subject of local lore, and in turn much of the myths of the area seep into people's collective consciousness, turning explainable shadows into ghosts. The truth might be somewhere in the middle, and at that crossroad lives the Redheaded Hitchhiker of Route 44.

For as long as people in the area can remember, there have been claims of a red-headed man walking down U.S. Route 44 in Rehoboth, Massachusetts, and some have stopped to pick him up only to have him disappear on them. It sounds like an excellent story, giving people chills around a campfire, but the story might be more truth than legend and the ghost might be more supernatural than literary.

The description of the ghost is always the first thing that draws people into the story. A driver is going along Route 44 at night, usually near the Seekonk-Rehoboth line when they encounter a well-built man between the ages of forty-five and fifty-five. He has red hair and usually a beard and is dressed in a red flannel shirt with either jeans or brown work pants and work boots. Sometimes he is well kept, but other times he appears disheveled with an overgrown beard, dirty pants, and an un-tucked shirt. He mostly appears solid to the drivers, but not quite all there while there are other stories where he is transparent throughout the entire encounter.

The biggest discrepancy in the physical description of the hitchhiker is with his eyes. Some say they look normal but just don't feel right. Some say they are black and empty; others, glowing and lifeless. Every color has been attributed to them at one time or another, from yellow and red to green, and it is this inconsistency that adds fuel to the skeptic's argument against the existence of a genuine spirit on Route 44.

While the man's look might draw people in, it is the stories of his exploits that keep people coming back. There is something about them that rings familiar, but like many things in the Triangle, there is a twist. There are many variations of the story, making him either a complex spirit or the subject of a town's imagination. Someone is driving along the road, usually alone, when they see the man on the side of the road. They stop to pick him up and the hitchhiker gets into the passenger or the back seat. He remains silent, ignoring questions and often staring at the good Samaritan. He eventually vanishes before their eyes or is no longer there when they turn to look. This is usually followed by some type of audio finale where he laughs, yells, or taunts them.

There are other tales attached to the mysterious man. Much like some of the stories from Freetown, there are also tales of people who drive through him...only to find no evidence of an impact when they stop. Others have seen him on the side of road, vanishing into the woods, or waving and disappearing. Still others have been scared to see him outside their car window while they were traveling at high speeds or have him suddenly be in their backseat.

Anyone who has driven that stretch of road at night can understand the uneasy feeling that pervades Route 44. A similar scene plays itself out in any rural town across America where there are more legends than streetlights. It is a classic movie set up, which may have something to do with the appearance of the spirit.

The earliest written record of the occurrence was set down by Robinson in the book *The New England Ghost Files*. He describes several encounters in detail. In one, the hitchhiker is seen outside the window of a fast moving car. Another person picked him up, only to have him vanish from the car. The most disturbing story in his book tells of a couple who broke down at about 10 p.m. The woman stayed in the car while the man went to get help. They both suffered separate experiences. The man saw him on the side of the road and tried to talk to him. The red headed man began yelling at him and then disappeared, laughing from all directions as the man made his way back to the car. The woman heard his voice come over the radio, taunting her until she ran from the car.

Townspeople have mixed feelings about their resident ghost. In a town known for its many hauntings, the hitchhiker is the most asked about. Law enforcement hates the attention, and the investigators it brings to the town, but some residents embrace it. Asking a local merchant will get you another story, usually beginning with the preface that it did not happen to him and it was a few years back.

Not all the stories are told in past tense. One woman claims she saw him walking into the woods on another road. She describes him differently and claims he never had red hair, but rather he died on another road with the color red in it, most likely, Redway Plain near Wilmarth Bridge Road. She says a

The town line of Rehoboth and Seekonk:
the haunting ground of the Red Headed Hitchhiker

local farmer died on that road after getting hit by a car while changing a tire for a stranded motorist. None of this has been able to be confirmed.

Chris has an uncomfortable relationship with the ghost. He first read Robinson's book when he was younger, and became so interested he contacted the writer to talk about the story. He eventually lost the book and recently bought it again when the price had come down on a website. He knew some of the history of the road, and had seen two people die on different parts of it over the years.

"I've made several attempts to try to reach the phantom but have come up dry each time, although strange things did happen. The first inspection resulted in a tire exploding when there was nothing visible on the road that could've popped the tire. The second instance was when my car stalled for a few minutes due to overheating." He says there was nothing wrong with his car before reaching that stretch of road.

He has all but given up looking for the ghost because of what happened the first time after his tire blew. "While waiting for a tow truck driver we were hearing noises most of the night. There was rustling and we thought it was the wind. It didn't sound like an animal and we heard walking. We didn't want to turn the radio on because the story says he can talk through that. We turned the radio and our cells off. It was scary. I had read the story when I was 7 or 8 and it creeped me out enough. To be that close was too much. The truck came and then the rustling just stopped. We were eager to get going."

While he can explain all of that away, another time driving down Route 44 makes him put more weight in the stories he hears from others. "I traveled down that strip of road again. It was late and I had fallen asleep as my other friend drove. She stopped short and was panicking. I woke up startled and confused. She said she thought she hit someone and we looked around to see no one in sight. Then I recognized where we were. I told her to get going and not to ask questions. To my surprise the car didn't start right away and after the third try it did. We drove off and I explained to her about the Red Headed

Phantom and she flipped, claiming the man she thought she hit looked like the ghost I had described."

Another woman named Alice claims she and her friends saw the ghost. "Some of us snuck out one night and walked down that whole road all the way to the railroad tracks. We think that we saw him. We all did. Let me tell you, when we saw that misty figure in the shape of a man, we bolted down that road back to the house as fast as we could." While Alice and her friends might have seen something, maybe even a ghost, it is only the location of the sighting that connects it to the hitchhiker. According to research, he has never been seen as just mist.

Wanda became interested in the history of the ghost after having seen him in her car one night. She was alone and saw him in the rear-view mirror. The radio started to scan the stations and then became so loud it shook the car. The man disappeared and began to laugh on the radio. "I looked into it, but I found nothing about him. Who this guy is...is a mystery. Why he is here is a mystery."

Stories like this are not unusual. Like a highway boogeyman, the hitchhiker takes the blame for every unexplained happening on the road. Then there are those natural things made to feel more supernatural given the history of the ghost. The explainable leaps into part of the lore, and witnesses become convinced before rational thought can enter the question.

It feeds the mythos of the story. Most of the modern stories about the phantom come from second and third hand sources. People retell them as true, almost as if it had happened to them. Recently people claiming to have seen the ghost have posted reports on the Internet. The majority of these can be discounted because the information seems to be a compilation of the rumors heard. Most do not get the town or physical description right.

The stories also start to feel like urban legends. Melanie has never seen the ghost before, but she says the story travels with her and her friends when they drive around. "Here are some things I have heard from reliable sources about a hitchhiker in Rehoboth. Apparently what happens is if you have three people in the car and one empty spot in the backseat he supposedly appears in the vacant seat for awhile, and then vanishes. The second thing is a bit more frightening. The driver will look over at the passenger in the front seat and see the hitchhiker. Upon his disappearance, the passenger will have no recollection of what happened. The second one happens more frequently than the first. Still, I haven't heard enough information to be comfortable going there. I'm sure something does happen, I just don't want to be put in a potentially dangerous situation." The stories do not stop her from driving the stretch of road though.

One of the last stories told about the hitchhiker is almost textbook urban legend. John has never had an encounter with a ghost, but his brother's friend had the air taken out of his lungs by something he saw on the road. "He had been driving alone when he saw him on the side of the road. He stopped and called out to the man who started to walk towards him. As he got closer, he faded until he had completely disappeared." This sounds like it may be true, but John goes on to tell how to invoke the spirit. "See, he had driven to the town line. They say if you drive to the town line, turn off your lights and honk three times, he will appear in your car or in your headlights when you turn them back on. This guy had tried that, but it didn't work. I guess the ghost was slow that night."

Stories like this make the believer in us nod our heads and avoid roads. They make the skeptics laugh. Every state has something like this, they say, and despite dozens of sightings over the decades, there is no documented proof other than first hand stories of the encounters. There are psychological and physical alternatives to the hauntings, as well an entire cannon of myths and urban legends utilizing the basic motif of the lonely road and the hitchhiker or traveler. Yet just because something can be explained doesn't mean it has been.

Most hauntings like the red headed hitchhiker have fallen into the realm of local legend, told as cautionary tales and local color. The most famous of these is Resurrection Mary in the Chicago area that has been reported in books and television shows such as "Unsolved Mysteries." Mary was a teenage immigrant who was killed in a car accident while coming home from a dance. She is still seen in her dress traveling the road between the hall and the cemetery at which she is buried trying to get home. She is often picked up and has been known to interact with the people who do so. She asks to be dropped off near the cemetery and vanishes near it or from the car as it passes.

If this sounds familiar, it should. Most states and several countries on both sides of the ocean have adopted it. There have been similar occurrences in other parts of the country including Kentucky, St. Louis, North and South Carolina, and Arkansas. Hawaii has a long history of hitchhikers vanishing, and for a long time it was thought to be the volcano god Pele who stole rides with horsemen and drivers. All have some twist unique to that area of the country and all are built upon first hand reports later spiced up and allowed to fall into myth and exaggeration.

These stories might be part of a broader tradition that continues to grow. Jan Brunvard, the most decorated folklorist in modern times, has written extensively on the topic of the vanishing hitchhiker, even naming one of his collections of urban legends after the tale. It is one of the most popular urban legends and seems to stretch across different times and cultures. New variants are being added every year. Some stories have a man picking a girl up and dropping her off at her house only to find her no longer in the car. When he approaches the door, the people inside tell him that it was the ghost of their daughter who died years ago on that stretch of road. Often there is a picture of the girl so the driver can identify her. Another has two men or a group of men picking her up and bringing her to the prom. They dance with her all night, noticing how cold she feels, before she vanishes. There is often proof left behind, like a scarf or a jacket left on a gravestone.

Another whole string, more in line with the hitchhiker on Route 44, has a man being picked up or just appearing in the backseat. He often has something prophetic to tell the driver that comes true and is sometimes Jesus himself.

One of the most disturbing tales is of a naked woman seen lying in the road in California. The driver gets out, but she is no longer there. Despite a search and the help of police, there is no one found. After three nights of sightings, they finally find her car off the road and hanging off an embankment. She is dead inside, but her son is still alive, hanging on to the last moments of life.

Our time and place does not have exclusive rights to the hitchhiker tales. Mythology from England and Ireland has its own version of the tale that dates back hundreds of years. *The Fortean Times* has published dozens of accounts, sometimes with a supernatural creature such as a vampire, werewolf, or black dog filling in. A famous British politician once saw his doppelganger on such a road. Irish fairy tales tell of people straying from the road only to fall into a fairy circle that causes disaster to befall them. There are tales from Roman days of walking along the road and encountering some supernatural being.

There is an account in the Bible, and the Devil is known to appear at crossroads to strike deals for hapless victims' souls. We are taught this connection between crossroads and evil early. A recent children's book explores the alphabet by using American traditions that go from A to Z. V is for Valley Forge and W is for the White House. X is for the Crossroads where Robert Johnson sold his soul.

The connective tissue of these stories is the lonely road and the unknown, and these symbols resonate with the reader because they are common and universal. Roads have long been associated with life; the path of our lives, the journey we must take. They also imply the soul is still traveling, never able to get where it needs to go. Are these just motifs of our collective unconscious or is there some basis for these localized hauntings? Myths might point out the archetypes of the traveler trying to get home and the obstacles he must overcome: the lonely road, dark turns, isolation in the woods. The very location of these hauntings allow our minds to wander and sends us crawling to our bedrooms as children where we shrink back from the darkness of our closed closet and underneath our bed. We see the crosses on the sides of roads and maybe even know the names and this adds to our tension.

Michael White offers another theory in his 1999 book *Weird Science: The Unexplained Explained by Science*. He writes about hypnagogic and hynopomic hallucinations and claims it explains away the majority of the hitchhiker stories. During long drives at night, especially in dark, secluded places, we tend to fall asleep. The repetitive scenery, the lull of the motor, and the constant yellow or white lines in the road put us in a hypnotic state that simulates the beginning and ending stages of sleep when we begin to enter a type of dream state. Our imagination is fed by the stories we hear about an area or the cliché environment we are in and we see things that are not there. People have even been known to interact and feel physical sensations during this stage of sleep.

Alan Alves describes the active mind and the creative mind. The creative mind is our subconscious where all of our memories are stored. This kicks in when we are driving through places we have traveled before, much like the local residence that represent the bulk of the reported sightings. This part of our brain takes over, which is why we often get home and do not remember anything about the trip. During this time our imagination takes over. We can create very real monsters and ghosts to fill the time, although Alves also admits that we may also be open to the paranormal that exists while in this state.

With mounting evidence against the possibility of the existence of the redheaded hitchhiker is there any evidence that he does exist? Back roads are primed for paranormal occurrences. People often suffer tragic accidents or die in violent ways in these rural settings without streetlights and quick turns that cannot be seen until you are on top of them. Does this particular legend just sound like an established bit of folklore, or is the folklore based on activity that is more common on roads than other places?

Folklorists look for similarities in stories when they create motifs and variants, but evidence of the existence of the hitchhiker in Massachusetts might be gained by looking at what is different in these tales. If you look at the reports before the area was modernized, some things stick out. First, most of the people reporting the occurrences did so with no alterative motive, and most of the people Robinson interviewed were asked about a separate legend completely and offered the hitchhiker story. Next, many of the people had never heard the legend and did not know each other. At times, the phantom has appeared to more than one person, which would make a hallucination like the one White talked about near impossible.

Then there is the ghost himself. He seems unworldly, unlike the people often seen in urban legends. He offers no advice or prophetic promises. In fact, he doesn't talk. His goal does not seem to get home, but to scare and taunt. He also has appeared outside of cars moving over fifty miles an hour, which shows up in none of the urban myth research. Lastly, he comes from an area long known to have paranormal activity.

The first encounters may be true. The stories date back long before the Internet and before people from the outside started to come in looking to pick him up. The stories were probably met with a half nod when they were told. The original accounts were not farfetched and told by friends. Then the stories started to mix with movies and something someone had heard somewhere before. They became part of the town and people no longer remembered where they had heard the story. There is a ghost on the patch of road leading into Seekonk, but he is no longer the man people would recognize. Now only the legend of the ghost haunts the town.

The Other
Most Famous Ghost

D iane and her son had decided to spend the night as a way of bonding. Teenage sons and their mothers have a tough time trying to find common ground, but this was something they were both interested in: old crime stories and ghosts. The site was only a few hours away and was a part of their state's history, so it seemed like an easy decision.

They planned to travel to Fall River and stay at the Lizzie Borden Bed and Breakfast.

They considered themselves lucky to get Lizzie's old room and settled in, waiting for the next tour to start. Diane unpacked her bags while her son, Brian, went to the bathroom after the long ride. He came out a few minutes later...white as the Victorian sheets. While he was in there thinking about the murder and his own excitement at possibly seeing a ghost, the water faucet turned on by itself. He slowly walked out of the room, too scared to turn the water off, and into the hallway to get some air.

"He didn't go back in the bathroom, I'll tell you that." Diane and Brian laugh at it now, but at the time they both thought twice about their decision to stay. "But that was why we came out. That's part of it."

Later that night they heard a scream from the room next to theirs. A woman and her two daughters who had no idea of the history of their rooms had decided to still stay after hearing about the murders. "They came screaming out of their room. Wouldn't say what happened, wouldn't go back in. We didn't know what happened." The three women left to find another place to lodge, and again, Diane and Brian, although scared, decided to stay.

"I mean, why leave. That's why we came."

For the staff, fleeing customers was nothing new. It was part of the job, like changing the sheets or vacuuming the carpet. They had long become used to the look of fear in patrons' eyes and quick departures in the middle of the night: AT THE LIZZIE BORDEN BED AND BREAKFAST, TOUCHING THE PAST AND HAVING IT GRAB BACK ARE PART OF THE PRICE OF ADMISSION.

The three-story house at 92 Second Street in Fall River hides many things behind its walls. It hides the actions of a shrewd, frugal businessman who rose to wealth and power at the height of the Industrial Revolution and the relationship between the four women who lived with him. It hides the details of one of the most notorious crimes in American history, unsolved despite being revisited time and time again. Most of all, hidden within the decorated rooms and pear wallpaper, among the renovated walls and the exposed beams, waiting to be returned to their former glory, are ghosts.

Fall River, located in Bristol County in the Southeastern part of Massachusetts, has a long history of violence. Since its beginnings as part of Freetown, Massachusetts and the violence it saw during King Philip's War, through the growing pains and crime of the Industrial Revolution, through the drug and police corruption scandals of recent decades, Fall River has gained a reputation not deserved by the majority of its residents. One crime that stands out in the minds of people outside of the city brings undesired fame and waves of history seekers and paranormal investigators.

On August 4, 1892, Andrew Borden was discovered by his next-door neighbor, Adelaide Churchill. The body of Mr. Borden was in the downstairs sitting room, half standing, half sitting, and she rushed to the nearest person for help. By the time the police arrived, the body of his second wife, Abby, had been found upstairs in the second floor guestroom. Both had been killed by what appeared to be an axe or hatchet. Although the first blow was believed to kill each of them, their faces were continuously struck and Mrs. Borden was almost decapitated.

The song born of the crime shows the difference between the facts of the case and the mythology surrounding it. Abby Borden was in fact Lizzie's stepmother and was struck nineteen times, while her father, one of wealthiest businessmen in town, received eleven. News of the murder spread quickly, and soon the evidence began to mount against Lizzie. She was in the house, or at least on the premises at the time of the crime, and an investigation found she had tried to purchase poison at least twice in the days before the murder.

As the investigation continued, rumor mixed with fact and the circumstances surrounding the killings became clouded with conjecture and hearsay. Blood was discovered in Lizzie's underclothes and she had disposed of her outer garments. She had sent people away who had tried to see Abby that day. There was enough reason for her to want them dead, and not all of them were obvious or known at the time. Others are the subject of speculation and rumor. Abby and Lizzie fought all the time, and Mr. Borden was tight with his money, not allowing his two girls to spend freely. Over the years, other elements have been added to Lizzie's motives. Some say her father had sexually abused her, while others claim Abby had discovered she and Bridget were having an affair and had threatened to expose it.

There were enough holes in Lizzie's story to bring her to trial, but there were enough holes to be exploited by her expensive attorney and reasonable doubt was allowed to creep in. Ultimately, she was found not guilty and released. She remained in the community for a while, but eventually used her inheritance to move away after being rejected by the town at every turn.

To this day the murders remain unsolved and have become the subject of legend. Countless books have been released on the subject. Some claim to have absolute proof of Lizzie's guilt, but for every one that comes out condemning her, there is another acquitting her of the crime. Modern forensic psychologists and criminologists have reviewed the case; every detail, no matter how mundane, has been agonized over and debated, and with every new theory the murders take on an even stronger life.

Plays and operas have been made of Lizzie's story and a full-length feature film focusing on her was released in 1975. Elizabeth Montgomery, the actress who made her name as Samantha on "Bewitched" and who's statute stands only a two-hour drive away in Salem, became synonymous with the suspected killer, largely due to the ice cold stare and smile she gives as Lizzie at the end of the movie. Lizzie has appeared on television shows and even pops up in comic books from time to time. Then of course there is the nursery rhyme.

Regardless of whether she committed the crime, Lizzie has lived on, but recently that idea has become more literal.

The final character in the Borden story is the house itself. Its location helped raise suspicion about Lizzie because of the thick, hard to open door; the lack of access to the outside; and the bustling neighborhood. The three-story Victorian was the obvious result of money, but it reflected the attitude of its owner. It was practical and well positioned, but a family with the Bordens' wealth could have afforded a bigger, nicer home in a better section of town.

One of Lizzie's first acts of freedom was to relocate and leave the past behind her. The house switched hands several times as Fall River's glory came and went. The neighborhood

surrounding it changed over the next hundred years and the old Borden place adapted itself to the times. The barn where Lizzie had supposedly been during the murders was torn down and additions were put on to accommodate new businesses.

In 1994, Martha McGinn, who had lived there at different times growing up, inherited it. She knew the location and the legend surrounding Lizzie could make for an interesting business if marketed the right way. Renovations began in 1996 and the house was transformed back to its old self, down to the smallest details from the day of the murders. The walls were covered in pear design wallpaper to reflect Lizzie's favorite fruit, and little hatchet cookie cutters were made to serve the guests. A full mannequin, dressed in Victorian clothes, was placed in the front to greet patrons. McGinn began selling the history of the homicides, and business boomed.

Even McGinn was surprised by the response the new business received, especially from people outside of New England. People flocked from all over the world to stay where the famous murders had occurred and sleep on a piece of infamy. They chose one of eight rooms, all of which had some sort of history attached to it, and ate the same breakfast the Bordens' enjoyed the day of the murder. Most came believing Lizzie had done the crime, but others came to see if they could piece together the clues and solve the who-done-it themselves.

The business was bought by Donald Woods and Lee Ann Wilber in 2003. They had stayed there one Valentine's Day and shortly after saw it on the market. They decided to buy it because it was an established business with a strong reputation and potential. There was another reason for finding the bed and breakfast on Second Street so attractive—it was starting to get a reputation for more than its history.

In the late 1990s McGinn allowed herself to be interviewed for an episode of "Unsolved Mysteries"—as did past and present employees. She admitted to experiencing ghosts in the house long before it ever came into her possession. As a teen she had heard marbles being played in the unoccupied room above her bedroom, accompanied by children laughing. She also saw the figure of an old woman dressed in Victorian clothes that floated through the basement and then disappeared. A former employee told how she had been making the bed in the guestroom where Abby's body was found and turned to adjust something in the room. When she turned back, there was the impression of a woman lying on the bed.

The report was nothing new to employees and guests who had been experiencing things for years, but now the word was out and people began making reservations hoping to see something otherworldly. Eleanor has been working at the bed and breakfast for almost seven years as a tour guide and night manager. She knew the history of the house when she was hired, but had not heard any tales of the paranormal before signing on. She has experienced dozens of hauntings over the years and now considers them routine. "I used to think when you're dead, you're dead. That's the end of it. It's not." She hides her experiences unless asked, but she finds now the subject of the paranormal comes up almost daily.

During her time in the house, she has seen the woman in the basement, describing her much as McGinn did. She has felt an unseen hand push down on her shoulder and neck and hears voices just above a whisper when in the parlor. She often hears a cat shrieking from inside a room although none of the owners or staff has allowed one in. She once saw a mysterious mist rise from the kitchen into the parlor where she sat reading just feet from where Andrew's body was found. There was nothing on the stove and no one on the first floor with her. She felt she was not alone and called McGinn's mother for advice.

"She hung up. She didn't want to admit anything."

One night she was hosting a tour and turned on the coffee, like she did every night, before leading them into the basement. When she arrived back upstairs with the group, the coffee pot was full but cold. The light on the machine was on, but the machine itself was unplugged.

Lee Ann Wilber has also experienced things since becoming manager there. "Sometimes I know I'm not alone in the room." She has seen odd shadows and quick flashes of figures—and she's heard the same cat Eleanor has heard. "I'm not scared of the small things. I'm immune to them because they are part of the house."

It's not only the employees who have seen spirits during their time there. People often have experiences they cannot explain or ignore until someone brings it up. An upstairs guestbook invites people to share what has happened to them, and reading through its pages is like flipping through a gothic novel. The reports range from odd feelings and cold breezes, to objects moving, to the full figure of a man thought to be Andrew in the front parlor and one of a woman believed to be Lizzie on the front stairs. People are eager to tell what they have seen and add to the lore of the house, but others, usually those who do not know the stories going in, leave without asking for their money back.

One man went upstairs to sleep after having taken the tour, but was interrupted by a presence holding him down in the bed. "I was trying to fight it, but it was so strong you can't fight." After being held down for several minutes, he went down to the bathroom to freshen up. Lizzie had always had a passion for pears, and as he used the pear lotion, he felt the air change. "I could tell it didn't like me using the lotion." Later he was in his room and he heard a foreign voice inside his head. "It asked me what could be thrown but not caught. I thought for a moment and then the voice answered, 'Your voice.' Then it laughed like it said the funniest thing in the world. I never would have just thought that up and I had never heard it before."

Bree went to the Bed and Breakfast years ago on Father's Day with her parents, noting outside the irony of the visit. On the mantle there were two candlesticks, slightly off center. Her father adjusted them, and as they walked away all three heard a thump. "I looked down and [the candlestick] was at my feet." She has been there several times since, and each time she experienced a sickening feeling that only went away when she left. That time it was worse in the kitchen. "I had to put my head down and almost left the room."

Bernie had a much different experience, but one that has been whispered about by others. His was mostly a dream, but as he slept in the guestroom, he relived the murders in vivid detail. "The killer was a man, but he was dressed all in black. He was a large guy, at least six feet tall and over two hundred pounds. I watched as he went through the house, room to room, like he was stalking someone. I saw him kill Andrew, then Abby. He then went out the front door and I woke up. I know it wasn't real and that it doesn't mean I actually saw the killer. They say it didn't even happen like that and I was obviously thinking about it. But when I woke up he was in the room. I couldn't see his face, but I could see him like a shadow. Then he walked towards the door, opened it, and walked out. I know I wasn't asleep anymore because I stood straight up and followed him out. There was nothing there."

Wilber and Woods now promote the paranormal aspect of the Bed & Breakfast, but said they had to feel it out before committing to it. McGinn had initially discouraged them from it during their tour, but now it makes up a good deal of their business. "I estimate about a third of the people come here to see a ghost, maybe more," says Wilber. Another third comes for history and to try and solve the murder and the rest come because of the location and accommodations. Recently the owners have allowed the television shows "Ghost Hunters" and "Haunted Travels" to shoot in the house, and after each broadcast they find the number of people interested in seeing the ghosts goes up. They also have ghost hunting classes sponsored by Haunted Times there several times a year, and have used the controversial Frank's Box in different rooms with varying results.

If the question of who killed Andrew and Abby has not been answered, the mystery of who walks the house unseen will probably remain clouded as well. While most paranormal investigators agree the kind of trauma the house has experienced would create a perfect setting for the paranormal, amateur and professional investigators have been unable to get a definitive answer to who might be restless or trapped. Wilber believes only some of the hauntings are the handiwork of the Bordens and thinks there are other people there as well. "I think other owners of the house are here too. There have been other deaths in this house."

The three ghosts most often seen are Andrew, Lizzie, and the woman in the basement. Andrew and Lizzie make sense, but the old woman in Victorian clothes is more of a problem. Most who see her agree that she does not look like Abby, which has led to the popular theory that she is Bridget, the housekeeper. This seems unlikely. Bridget was a young woman at the time of the murders and did not stay on until old age. Her ghost returning to the site of a tragedy as an elderly figure does not fit with other haunted stories.

The other experiences in the house remain unsolved as well. Who turned the coffee off and touches Eleanor on the shoulder? Who were the children McGinn heard as a teenager?

On November 11, 2005, renowned psychic Jackie Barrett was asked to come and try and contact whatever spirits might be lurking at the B&B. Barrett, known for her work as a life coach with athletes and her work in New Orleans, felt a presence in the house as soon as she arrived. "It's a guest house. You come in and out, but I feel like I'm intruding." As she got ready for the ceremony, a chair in her room moved.

During a séance she contacted the spirit of Bridget—whom she felt strongly as she toured the house. The spirit channeled through one of the guests, and though she wanted to speak, she did not like being called out and forced to talk to the group. No words were said, but the woman who volunteered...her face and demure changed during the entire ritual. The mood of the room changed, and it seemed the woman was going to lash out at Barrett at any moment. Several people became sick during the hour of communication and more broke out in rashes and hives after.

Barrett felt that Bridget had been involved with the murder of the Bordens, even if not directly. She felt very close to Lizzie and wanted to protect her, but the well trained psychic was unable to determine if she had killed them herself to protect Lizzie or had helped her cover it up.

Like many aspects of the case, the facts often contradict themselves. Bridget was sick the day of the murder, but could have helped in the killings, although she was generally considered close to the parents and not fond of Lizzie at all. In fact, Lizzie and her sister often called her Maggie, the name of their old maid as if servants were all the same and did not warrant individuality.

Barrett's part in the story might not end there. Shortly after her visit to the house, a spirit made contact with a new member of the staff. The high school student had a book drop at his feet, and believing it to be the ghost of some of the children rumored to haunt the building, began reading to them whenever he worked. The book was Barrett's *The House that Kay Built*, a collection of her experiences as a psychic. The teenager had never met the woman and did not know she had recently been there. Something in the house is reaching out to an expert who can talk to it.

That is the way it is in the Fall River Bed & Breakfast. Trapped between a past that no one will ever truly know and a present mixed with mystery lies the spirits of those who have shared a small plot of land and a place in history. Recent renovations had hoped to discover the murder weapon or some new evidence, but like everything in the Borden case, things never quite make themselves clear.

People will go on asking questions and searching for the answers. Another dimension has been added to the enigma at 92 Second Street, and while the street, the neighborhood, and the city have moved on, the house remains trapped. The ghost inside may be able to look out and see the changing world, but its cries and screams go unheard. If the only thing that may free the ghosts inside is the truth, they may never find peace. Lizzie and her family hide their secrets well.

Part Five

IN SESSION

Walking the Halls of the Triangle

I n Lawrence, Massachusetts, a new school rose from the ashes of an old one. Like many things in Massachusetts, the building that once housed St. Mary's Catholic High School was reopened as Notre Dame High School. With only three grades and small numbers, the community needed something to bring it together. The English teacher, a fan of good legends and ghost stories, invented one involving a young Dominican girl who was accidentally hung after slipping off the roof during a rainstorm. The story was made up to give the school a sense of tradition because every school needs a ghost.

Her cries could still be heard, and her shadow seen hanging on certain nights. She is said to be responsible for a pencil that rolled down the steps one night, and one teacher reported hearing her walking on the third floor late one night while he worked correcting papers. There is no young Dominican girl who died, but students feel her all the time and hear her in the girl's bathroom. Some have even seen her walking up the stairs. An investigation was actually conducted there and evidence gathered, including an EVP of a female voice with an accent saying, "I'm here."

All of this points to a central issue in who we are as people. With so many people going through them, schools are like archives of our history. The halls begin to buckle from the generations that walk down them, and each new yearbook adds more chapters to the story. We expect them to be haunted, and the story is passed down from the older students to the younger. The back-stories are often the work of urban legends, but that doesn't mean ghosts do not walk into the classroom.

Fairhaven High School

Fairhaven High School may be the most haunted school in the Triangle. The hauntings there have reached the status of legend to everyone outside the town. Those who attend tell the stories of upperclassmen who have seen chairs move and lights go on and off on their own. Called the Castle on the Hill, the school is the perfect setting, especially when you consider it was originally built in the 1800s. A man, believed to be the ghost of Henry Huttleston, the town benefactor, has been seen walking through the walls at night. The man has also been reported to be baffled by water bubblers, giving weight to the idea he is an intelligent spirit and not just a residual haunting. Students often see lights in the building flashing when they pass the school late at night.

Tabor Academy

Tabor Academy in Marion is known as one of the most exclusive and proper institutions in the state. That does not stop it from being haunted. The back-story involves a boy who killed himself at Lillard Hall. Cries and noises are heard late at night still, like he is debating whether or not to kill himself, and then the screams as he does. Many who attend the school have heard the story, but no one remembers the name of the student or has ever met anyone who actually heard the noises. Several do report seeing a shadowy figure on the athletic fields. While it might not be unusual to see someone out late at night, especially with a high number of students boarding at the school, the person is not a resident who pays tuition. The figure is said, however, to glow in the dark with an eerie green light and to disappear when approached.

Heather saw the figure, which she calls the Black Man, late in the year in 1995. "He was in a flowing cape and I thought it was someone dressed like the Grim Reaper. I yelled out that Halloween was over, and he turned. There was no face and it faded out, like the screen at the end of the movie. People told me they had seen it too."

Bridgewater State College

Perhaps the most haunted school in the Triangle is the one that bears its name. Bridgewater State College has been one of the better-known haunted schools in Massachusetts for over twenty years. It seems only fitting for a school just down the road from the swamp and a stone's throw from the state hospital that still stands as a beacon for the supernatural. Students are just trying to get an education, among other common college experiences, but the OTHER SIDE will not leave well enough alone.

There seems to be a higher interest in the paranormal in school-age teens and young adults. It builds from the early teens, coming off of old ghost stories and leading to true hauntings, and gains momentum in early adulthood. Perhaps it has something to do with youth and their mastery of every new technology that comes along, but more college students are online willing to share what they have experienced and get the word out about the wraths from their campus. At times it feels like a competition.

The ghost stories come in floods. There are the well-publicized stories of George, mostly associated with the campus auditorium. He plays with the sounds and lights during rehearsals and shows. There is the phantom horse seen on the athletic field that runs in circles and disappears. There are the prerequisite suicides and murders and the covering up of tragedy by the administration to keep the school in business. Everyone knows the stories, but few have one of their own to tell.

The most haunted building on campus may be Shea-Durgin Hall. Almost since its construction, there has been an unusual energy present. There are rumors of a ghost on the third floor of the dormitory that has all the characteristics of a poltergeist. Things end up missing, and people have been said to find things stacked. Chairs, books, and cans have all been found to be piled one on top of each other instantaneously, something impossible to do as evidenced by the number of inebriated college students who have attempted it with beer cans in the dorm. There is also a story about a murdered coed who was strangled and left naked by her jealous boyfriend. Today students still hear his yelling at her and her cries. They also hear her sobbing. At night females have been woken up by a tight feeling on their neck...as if they were being strangled by unseen hands.

For Ryan the hauntings were more than just some urban legend posted on ghost sites. What she experienced caused her to leave the school completely. "On my first day they told me all of those stories. I love a good ghost story and liked that my dorm was supposed to be haunted. You can't be in college and not have a haunted dorm. They go hand in hand."

In addition to the more popular stories, she also heard of the old man who had lived on the third floor. Although she could not remember why he had been there, he had died in his room and his ghost was seen in the two rooms next to the one he had lived in. There was the story of the suicide room on the fifth floor and the moving beds on the fourth. The whole place was haunted, but no one ever told her about the woman who tried to kill her.

"Almost all of them were told about other schools. During a trip to Wheaton I had heard the one about the old man; my boyfriend at Boston College had heard of a murdered girl. I just took it all in. Then in my first month I found I couldn't sleep. I would wake up at weird hours and hear crying. I thought it was one of my roommates, but I could never see them crying. Then I thought it was just my imagination."

Ryan asked around, but no one knew anything about the crying or heard it at night. Most people, including the resident assistant, laughed it off and asked her to keep it off the ghost websites. She was not laughing.

"It started to affect my schoolwork. I couldn't sleep and would almost pass out in class. Sometimes I would just wake up. Most times, I would wake up and hear something...a weeping or a full-blown cry. When I did sleep, and it was just a few hours, I would have horrible dreams where someone would be chasing me.

"Then I saw her. Just after my first midterms, which I failed, I was sleeping. It was maybe two in the morning and I was jolted from my sleep. There was a woman at the foot of my bed. She was probably in her mid-twenties and looked like Mia Farrow in "Rosemary's Baby." She was wearing a light tan raincoat and was either naked or wearing a short skirt because I couldn't see anything else."

The woman stared at Ryan for a few seconds and then crawled on top of her. She struggled, but she could not move enough to force the woman off. "She started to strangle me. I could feel her on me—and her hands on my neck. I started to black out and I don't remember anything else until the next morning."

When she woke up the next day, she had pain in her neck and a slight red mark near her throat. She was frightened and demanded her room be changed or that she be sent to another dorm. When the college refused to listen, she dropped out and transferred schools.

"I know, it was a dream, right? Problem was I still had those marks on my neck and I was awake for a few minutes before she attacked me."

The Old Hag Syndrome is a fairly common theme in the paranormal. People wake up to find someone over them or on top of them who try to steal their air. It has been told and retold by different cultures for centuries, and has been explained away by sleep paralysis. It does not fit Ryan's story. In her experience, whatever tried to kill her came across a distance to get to the bed and then climbed on top of her. While her stress and lack of sleep may be to blame for the woman in the raincoat, she feels there was something else...something unexplained that was attracted to her for some reason.

"I tried to look into the girl, but found nothing. I think there was something in the building or the property that made her come to me. I don't know if she was the woman who was crying or the one who made her cry, but it was enough for me to leave."

Most school ghost stories are not as intense as Ryan's and while they linger, they do not still cause nightmares years after. Most are fun; part of the college experience and something that bonds the people together. As long as emotional teens and young adults gather together to learn, and as long as there are older students who can pass on tales to younger ones, like elders passing stories on to the youth over a fire, schools will continue to have their share of ghost stories. Most will never be true, although the people who hear them will argue that they are. In the collected lore there is a grain of truth, and for the student who momentarily touched that truth, there is more than literature and science to be learned in school.

Wheaton Ghosts

Wheaton has done more to promote the ghost on campus than most schools in the Bridgewater Triangle. Stonehill discourages Ouija Boards and dispels many of the stories told, and many of the high schools do not talk about them at all. At Wheaton, the ghosts are talked about and written about every Halloween. Perhaps it has something to do with its history as a female seminary or just because of its New England setting, but there's a sense of pride, and if the spirits are hard to pin down, they still have a long list of potential souls still trapped in Norton.

The stories begin with Eve Everett, who dates back to the time when the school was still all girls. Different stories are told about how Everett died. Some say either a boyfriend killed her or a jealous friend, while the earliest reports say she committed suicide. Like many hauntings that have no probable story attached to them, Everett changes her death with the needs of the students who talk about her. There does seem to be some connection to water though. She is known to turn faucets and showers on and off and to sap the heat out of the water at will. The stories that speak of her as a murder victim say she was hung and could scratch as the life drained from her. This might be used to explain the odd scratching heard on doors and the ceiling at night.

On the lower campus is Clark Hall. Many of the students feel the building's namesake haunts the dorm because several of them saw an old man in their room. They refused to live in the room anymore and now the school has such a hard time killing the rumor of the mysterious man they have to keep it empty to satisfy the other students.

Ghost stories often combine motifs. At Mary Lyon Hall, a building primarily used for alumni services and meetings, two of the classic themes of hauntings live together. In the building two mix-matched lovers replay the tragedy of their torn romance on a loop, but their background is the haunted school, the place they first met and fell in love. Perhaps that is the only place their passion could have existed. He was a resident of Norton and she was a student whose rich parents disapproved of the affair. The story plays itself out. They were set to meet and she was delayed. He waited all night in the freezing cold for his angel, only to die of exposure. Time continues to keep the two apart. People report hearing the lost man calling for her at night in the building. She never answers.

Perhaps the enduring quality of these stories is their ability to touch all of the emotions we feel, especially those felt by the young college students who still feel love so strongly they would wait out in the cold until they died for their infatuation. There is even a touch of *Withering Heights*, still taught in the literature classes, in the story. Real or not, the sightings, or in this case the hearings, persist.

No greater passion can be felt by some than those feelings set aside for man's best friend. There are many stories of ghost pets, but most involve the former owner who still experiences his canine friend. At Wheaton, the owner lives on, and among the many reports of his ghost walking the campus, there is the one of him looking for his faithful dog.

Wheaton enjoyed a time of expansion during the presidency of its first leader, Dr. Samuel Valentine Cole. In his spare time, he walked the campus with his faithful dog, Sandy. The two cannot be separated by death. While he has been known to be seen in the different buildings he helped raise funds for, like the admissions office, he is most known as the man behind the disembodied voice that calls out Sandy's name. He has also been known to open and close the chapel door and call the dog's name, as if Sandy has entered the building and he is going after him.

"I was waiting one night and it was pretty cold," says Jackie, a student at the college in the late nineties. "I had heard some of the stories, but not about Cole and his dog. It was late October, sometime before Halloween. I was there and I heard a whistle and a soft voice calling something out. I couldn't hear what it was. I heard a rustle of the leaves, like someone was walking. I mean, it was right in front of me, and it wasn't the wind. Then I heard the name Sandy. I thought it said Andy actually, but someone told me the dog story and it made sense."

While there are some stories that persist at the school, like the ghost who returned from the dead to water plants that would not live on their own, or the hanging tree where the outcast committed suicide, the most well known phantom on campus has to be the old librarian, Mary Armstrong. Her spirit has become so connected to the school, alumni have returned to campus just to hunt for her ghost. The story goes that she joined the staff in the early 1920s and became overworked. She moved away to live with her sister, and for reasons unknown, perhaps the stress of the job she had just left, took her own life. She returned to her true passion though, and continues the job she both loved and hated.

According to a report by Jennifer Robertson in the October 27, 2004 edition of the school paper *The Wire*, there are many stories attributed to the former employee. A security guard named David Cordella saw an empty elevator, believed to be inhabited by Aunt Mary's ghost, run by itself. Marion Doro heard doors opening and closing in the library one night and then saw a short woman in an old coat that vanished before her eyes. There are many reports of cold spots in the building and lights turning on and off, and on rare occasions, people have seen her ghost.

Jacob only saw her legs. "I was studying at one of the tables, just about to fall asleep. I heard books banging, like someone stacking them, and heard a cart move. I looked and a book truck was moving behind the rows. It was ten feet away from me. I heard and saw the thing between the spaces in the books, and then I saw a pair of legs in a dress or skirt moving along with them. It stopped and I got my bag and got ready to take off. I walked by the row, and the cart was there and no one was with it. Whoever had pushed it wasn't there. There was no way she could have gone anywhere. I ran out and didn't tell anyone until today about it."

One of the more bizarre stories of Aunt Mary involves the group of alumni who came looking for her in 1979. They searched the library all night for her. According to Robertson, "The book *Between Life and Death* had seemingly been pushed off the stacks as each party walked by."

Wheaton College is not just a place for a good story on Halloween. The spirits are part of the culture, like skipping class and stressing about majors. It binds the years together—tradition passed on without question. It does not matter to the students in Norton that their ghosts sound like clichés to the outside, myths spread on every campus across the country. Someday the lovers may find each other and Cole may find his beloved dog. Maybe the dead, the suicides, and accidents, will find peace, but for now they are still part of the price of tuition.

Stonehill College:
Haunted Hotspot or Urban Legend?

Donahue Hall at Stonehill

Darla was staying late at the basketball courts waiting for a friend and taking a few shots at the basket. She missed every shot by a mile, banging the ball off the backboard or missing the hoop all together. Basketball was not her game. She heard a noise near the bolted door, something like a scratching, and moved over to it to see what it was. There was nothing, and the door was locked and secure. She heard a ball bouncing and looked over to see the basketball she had just shot and placed on the ground bouncing up and down, never reaching more than two feet high.

"It looked like a little kid was dribbling the ball, but there was nothing there. I watched it go up and down about five times, and it never lost momentum, so I know it hadn't fallen off the rack. I just stood there and after a while it stopped completely and rolled to my feet. I ran out of there like it was on fire and never went back into that building."

The haunting is nothing new. Stories like this have been coming out of the building for decades, but it is the reason for the ghost that raises interest. "I'm sure it was the little girl. She drowned there and her ghost haunts the place. I think she wanted to play and I invited her by playing first. She's trapped there all alone, and I think that's very sad. She was the daughter of one of the presidents, and that is why they don't have a pool at Stonehill."

That is what the ghosts are like at Stonehill College in Easton, only miles away from the Hockomock Swamp and one of two four-year universities near the heart of the Bridgewater Triangle. There are very real reports of phantoms there since the 1960s, not unusual for a northeastern Catholic college, but the stories are a blend of encounters and urban legend. There are ghosts at Stonehill College, but it is the legends that explain them that refuse to die. They are passed down from older students to the wide-eyed first year students too confused to know better, but there is something more. Students are introduced to their ghosts from one of the deans of the college and continue to hear them as they move from one dorm to another.

Take the story of the little girl. Darla's story is not unusual. There have been reports of little feet being heard on the stairs and a few sightings of a young glowing girl in a white dress running behind the furniture that now adorns Alumni Hall. The strong smell of chlorine hits people there late at night, and screams from a little girl are heard from the outside of the building, sometimes causing people to rush in and see if everything is okay. Students and faculty hear the details of the sightings and always know who the little girl is. Like Darla recited, the ghost is said to be the little daughter of one of the presidents of the college. It is often said that she was left unattended by her father, who was too busy to watch her, and slipped on the wet floor, hit her head, and fell into the pool, drowning. In his grief, her father had the pool filled and declared no pool should ever be built on campus again. The college obliged, first out of honor for such an influential man and then because it became part of the school's tradition.

There is no report of any little girl who lost her life on campus, and no one has ever died at Alumni Hall. More importantly, her drowning did not cause them to fill up the pool with cement and she was not the daughter of the president. Nicole Tourangeau makes her living keeping the stories of the school alive. She runs the school archives and knows the tales better than anyone. "I don't know where the whole president's daughter thing started. We had never heard that. All our presidents have been priests."

In reality, the pool existed at the school until the fall of 1951. The college decided to admit women, and had no faculties for them on that side of the campus. The pool was sacrificed and the area became a coed student lounge. Later basketball hoops were added, and sometime later the legend started.

The ghost is sometimes said to be that of Mary Calendar Ames, the daughter of the Ames family who brought the college to prominence and who is the subject of many of the hauntings at the school. She was one of four children and some believe she is actually the one who died in that tragic accident. This story is usually used when the tale of the president's daughter is shot down. Ames is as unlikely a victim seeing she died in her old age in another part of the state.

Colleges breed these kinds of stories, and most schools tolerate them or spend time and energy trying to rid the campus of the ill-conceived rumors. This is not the case at Stonehill. While they work to make sure people know the school is not haunted, even going so far as to write letters to editors of the papers that print the ghost stories as true and get the details wrong, they embrace the urban legends surrounding Stonehill. Dean Dick Grant runs a tour detailing them and showing students and their parents some of the lesser-known corners of the college. According to him, the stories build a sense of community and make the history of the school, and the people who help build it, come alive for the next generation. "People make it up as they hear it. Then it takes a life of its own. It takes on a reality. They need it. It's crucial to have a sense of history. What is our connection to the past?" He claims all the stories are false, but the mythology was strong enough to make it into a report on ghost stories published by John Hopkins University.

Nicole Tourangeau feels the same way. As the university archivist, she is the keeper of the history of Stonehill, which also makes her an authority on the ghosts stories told there. "For some reason the stories persist. The students hear them as incoming freshmen. Anytime I do a talk, I try to dispel the myths. Even when you tell the students it's not true, some don't want to know. Many times the story is passed down from older siblings, but the college itself is guilty of feeding the legend. It gets reprinted in the school newspaper."

One story that often gets reprinted is the story of the ghosts of O'Hara Hall. According to a report in the school's paper *The Summit*, Thomas O'Brien was a student there in 1965. He awoke one night to see a blurry figure standing over him. The ghost was wearing an old fashion pilot's uniform and had no face. O'Brien, now a local businessman, shot under his sheets and when he pulled them back down, the man was gone. The same haunting has occurred in other rooms in the dorm and the reports get written every Halloween in *The Summit*. There was even an exorcism done in the dorm to get rid of the dark man.

The figure is thought to be the spirit of Freddy Ames, the eccentric son of the founder who died in a horrible plane crash on campus. His passion for flying forced them to build a runway that still exists on campus. Who was in the plane that night remains a mystery and is part of the legend of the story. Some say his mistress died in the crash as well, and one of the most popular stories is that his pet chinchilla died with him and may have been the reason for the crash. According to stories, he was unharmed when they found him, except for his face. The engine was said to have exploded and burnt it clear off, accounting for the faceless ghost seen in the dorm. The reason he crashed is debated as well. One story says a servant, unhappy with his boss, forgot to turn the landing lights on, and Freddy, seeing the bright glow from the front rooms of the residence, now Donahue Hall, assumed them to be the runway and crashed into the hill. Another tale says the servant was drunk and forgot to light the way, while another claims the mysterious woman flying with Freddy was the servant's wife and he decided in his jealousy to get rid of both the guilty parties. Even the faithful dog has been blamed for the accident because he bit his owner's leg at just the wrong time.

This story, like almost all of the neatly packaged ones flying around the school, is far from true. Freddy did love flying, crashed on campus often, and did die in a crash. The site of his demise, however, was miles away in Randolph, Massachusetts. "He did crash his plane here, but it was not the fatal crash," says Tourangeau. "I usually tell our students to feel free to think the ghost of Freddy haunts Stonehill College as long as they understand he is looking for his way home to Randolph." The story was published in the paper and made its way onto a local talk show, only to have a family member call the president of the school and complain. Although it led to a better relationship between the Ames' and the college, the school is always very quick to set the record straight that Freddy could not be haunting the dorm, even if they are not as quick to say there is no haunting at all.

In O'Hara dormitory there is reported activity. "I never saw a guy in a pilot hat," says Frank, who graduated in the spring of 2006. "We talked about the hauntings there though. People joked you shouldn't bring anything valuable there because it would vanish. I don't mean stolen. I mean, you turn around and your watch or keys were gone. A paper due in an hour or a book you need to read. It happened to me at least once a week, and you'd have to say, 'Freddy, can I have my watch back?' You'd leave the room, come back, and it would be on your bed."

Frank never saw a figure in the night, but says other people have and do not like to talk about it. "It happens a bit, but we talk about it between us and not people on the outside." O'Hara also has a reputation for things moving on their own. There has never been anything malicious, but there is enough to keep people on their toes.

The real haunting might be outside the dorm. The pond is said to be the place of the crash, another myth seeing its

O'Hara Hall — perhaps the most haunted building on campus

distance from Donahue, and that an odd fog appears on the anniversary of the crash. The haunting has made it onto numerous paranormal websites and gets reprinted in the Boston newspapers. The bluish smoke has a mind of its own, moving across the pond, creeping onto the land, and then retreating again. The body of water is actually three connected ponds, with the larger being the main one and the other two used to collect and retain water. The whole campus is very wet and in the valley of an actual hill, hence its name, so the fog might be a natural occurrence.

Other places on campus are said to be haunted. Pictures taken in the teaching assistant room always have bright orbs in them. People hear things moving and see lights in Donahue hall. Like many college campuses, the use of the Ouija board is banned. After hearing some of the stories, and hearing several students in his dorm waking up to see figures in their rooms and being unable to move, Harry tried one in his friend's bathroom. They shut off the lights in Bernallia's dorm and prepared to talk to the other side. They played for a while; nothing happened, so he went back to his room. "Later on we were sitting in my friend's room and the TV was off. Then, all of a sudden, it went this strange maroon color, like blood, on the screen." The television was not on, and the color went away as quickly as it appeared. It scared both of them, and they vowed never to use the board again.

The board also helped discover the name of one of the ghosts in the Seminary, or the Sem as people on campus call it. Several students using the Ouija made contact with a spirit that called himself Ned. It was unclear what his connection to the school was, but he claimed to have been there since the 1950s and liked to look after the students to make sure they were okay. Ned has a preference for the female students.

Ned only touches the surface of the activity at the Sem. Originally used as housing for the priests on campus and students who wished to join the seminary, the building is now mainly a freshman dorm. Underneath the building are a series of passageways that the students refer to as the catacombs. "It's pretty scary down there," says Dan Grant. "You can go all down these corridors and not know where you are. I wouldn't be surprised if there are stories about it." There are. Students have said they see shadows moving in the dim light of the passageways. They hear scratching against the wall, but there is a rhythm to it that makes them feel it's not a rat or another animal. There are tales of students going down there and never coming back up...and of bones found in the darkness.

Most of the hauntings revolve around what might be buried there. From the bottom floor, the pattern near the main entrance of the dorm suggests something was closed up, hidden from people who might be curious. In reality, the difference in the title does cover something; an old fountain no longer in use. That is not what the students say however. According to most legends, there used to be a stairway leading to the catacombs underneath, and priests and students of honor who died were buried there to keep them close to home. Some say you can see them appear in the moonlight, coming up through the floor and walking outside, perhaps to a nearby cemetery.

The legend of the buried bodies is false, but that has not stopped something from haunting the Seminary, now a residence, retreat center, and the launching ground of the campus ministry. "I had heard the building was haunted," says Jonathan, who attended the school in the late 1980s. "I think there is a connection there for the priests. I woke up one night to find a man standing over me. I don't know why, but I thought he was a Father. There was a look about him that screamed priest. Maybe it was the bald head and the little glasses." Jonathan feels the man wanted to say something to him because his smile turned to a frown and he started towards the door.

"He started to leave and I sat up and asked him if I could do something for him. I don't know why, but I wasn't scared at all. He turned around. I actually stopped a ghost in his tracks. He smiled again and then shrugged and went through the door. He didn't open it, he just walked through."

A similar man has been reported by several other students, although no one can track down who he is. He has become just another phantom of the campus, seen and remembered as truth for only as long as the student who saw him is still on campus. People also talk of a dark figure, more negative in nature, and whispers heard through the walls at night. There has also been a young woman who has been seen in mirrors and reflective glass throughout the building.

One of most unusual tales told about the campus has nothing to do with ghosts. Cattle were big business during the height of the Ames wealth and influence. They were known to own some of the finest bulls and leased them out at a hefty price to farmers looking to guarantee the highest quality beef. Out of respect and honor, each prized beast was given a proper burial in a bull graveyard. The only trouble is no one knows where it is now. Somewhere on campus, more than a half dozen animals rest in peace.

The same might not be said for the people buried on the southwestern part of campus, slightly south of the Sem. People walking home at night have seen an unnatural fog waft through the area and travel to the cemetery. Others have seen a man, seen only as a shadow, in the graveyard standing and looking towards the middle of campus. He is seen for only a moment and then vanishes.

Matt knows what he saw because he was of a clear mind and was not suffering from a delusion, too little sleep, or an overactive imagination. It was also only a few minutes past noon. "I had an early class and was walking to the fields. I was actually walking pretty fast because I was late meeting this girl there. Neutral site. I went by the cemetery a bit away from it. I saw a young kid, maybe about sixteen, walking in. He was wearing a nightshirt, which made me feel something was up. People wear their PJs all the time on campus to class, but this was an old fashion nightshirt, like a guy dress. He should have been wearing one of those long hats.

"Anyway, I called out and the kid stopped. I said something about what he was wearing, like that I liked it, and he seemed very distracted. He asked me if I knew what time Celia was expected in. Okay, that was weird. I didn't know anyone by that name and there was no one else around us. We were outside. I told him that and he just asked me again. I was like twenty feet from him. He wasn't transparent or anything like that. He was solid. He whipped around and started running into the cemetery. When he entered, he just faded away. It was so quick it looked like he just disappeared, but now that I think about it more, he faded."

Like many things in the Bridgewater Triangle, the odd energy on the campus of Stonehill might be connected to the Wampanoags, King Philip, and the war. In the hidden areas of the property, and on the adjacent land, there are several caves and boulder formations where it is believed the Wampanoags lived. They resided there since their settlement of the area, but it is believed they used them during the war as hide-outs and bases of operation. It is known they used the area, and that Philip and his generals considered some residents in Easton hands off. Artifacts found on campus point to a possible Native American cemetery on campus, and some bodies have been found. In addition, there have been tools and odd black spots recovered by researchers.

That might be the cause for the lights on campus near the hill. Some have seen orbs of light, from a few inches in diameter to more than a foot, floating and moving towards the caves. At least two people have seen two or more lights moving together, almost like one is following the other. There is no sure answer for where the burial ground – if there is one – might be on campus, but it is rumored King Philip stayed in the caves during the war. The lights might belong to him or one of his followers checking to see if he is still in hiding. With so many locations claiming the ghost of Philip, it might be more wishful thinking than historical accuracy, but so much at Stonehill depends on the slight distortion of the past.

The story is what matters. Things are moving and voices are being heard at Stonehill College, but for every story there is a motif in urban mythology touched upon. People share their stories and speak of the hauntings happening to them at the most normal of times. Maybe that is the barometer to judge what is true on campus. The legends talk of buried bodies and dead children and mistresses being burned alive holding the family dog. Those stories always start with, "People say."

The true hauntings start with a hushed tone and begin with, "You're going to think this is weird, but…"

The sexy stories draw you in and tell you something is happening at the college. The more unexplained the haunting, the more you search for the reason and expect the bizarre as truth. In Easton, both types of stories are true, some are just truer than others depending on whom you believe.

And Then Again…

It is easy to pass off the stories at Stonehill. They make light of their spirits and tell stories as if the paranormal is an inherent

The pond where Lillie once saw a green mist. The mist has been reported for years.

birthright for a northeastern college, but there is nothing to be scared of. The ghosts are just the things of legend and nothing but a story. Enjoy them.

The same cannot be said for Lillie's experiences at the college in the early 1980s. She was a commuter who had graduated from high school at fifteen and was studying physics. She had grown up with the unexplained and had touched all the things that make the headlines in the Triangle. She had UFO and Bigfoot experiences while living in New Hampshire. As a child she would sit and listen to a ghostly phantom play the piano. "I had a lot of experiences growing up, so the paranormal was not really foreign to me."

Her studies brought out the atheist in her, and it was not until a friend of hers died during her junior year of undergraduate studies that she gave in to what had been a growing talent in her earlier years. She began to explore her skills and cultivate her psychic ability. "I was spending some time in the dark places and freaking my friends out. I could answer questions without them asking them out loud."

She also began to have more unexplained experiences that bled over to her daily life in school. She spent her early years at Stonehill confined to one side of campus, but that all changed her senior year. She spent more time near the Sem, which had changed its name to the Holy Cross Center by then. She knew about the ghosts of the college and had seen and heard several. She had seen the mist near O'Hara dorm and had heard drums playing near King Philip's caves. She had even seen the little girl inside the gym.

"I had heard stories, but you don't pay much attention to it until you experience it. I went to a little reception and I told my boyfriend I would help clean up. There were a few of us and no one else was around. I heard a ball bounce, but there was no ball there to be bounced. Then I heard a little kid laughing, and that's when I said, 'Okay, I'm leaving now.' It sounded like it was coming from the center of the place. It was female. The following day my friend told me about some girl who had died up there."

There is a trend with people who work with the darker forces within the paranormal. At some point well before they realize their calling, they come into contact with something that tries to stop them from getting into the field. Whether their victory over the evil force pushes them on or their retrospect gives them clarity, the person usually credits the experience with inspiring them to get into the work. Lillie is now a psychic and spiritual healer who has investigated the paranormal from Massachusetts to England and identifies herself as a person who can rescue ghosts. She credits her education at Stonehill with molding her life, but not because of what she learned at the belltower at the Holy Cross Center.

It was one experience in a year of unexplained things that drove her forward to start looking into alternative religions and psychic exploration. The scientist in her still prevails, and she takes a very reason-based approach to her spirituality. Her ideas on theoretical physics walk hand in hand with her belief in something more, and it all started with her uneasy feeling as she walked that part of campus.

"It was my last year there. I was spending a lot of time with my friends who lived at Holy Cross Center. I was there at all different hours. We kept getting really creepy feelings whenever we went by the belltower and into the chapel. Sometimes we would go into the chapel and look up at the balcony and see these glowing red eyes. We tried not to spend time there."

Little things began to happen when they spent any time there. "One time I went and the lights in the hallway went out one by one. I could just feel something not good coming from where the chapel was." She felt she could not avoid it and that there was something pushing her forward towards what was living in the tower.

"I felt like I was avoiding the whole area near the Center and just wanted to confront it and get it over with. One night I had the bright idea to confront it. I went in there by myself, turned the lights on, and I started screaming at whatever was there to show itself. I saw the two glowing red eyes high in the balcony and [they] started to come towards me. I could see the outline of this energy thing. It was coming towards me and I was freaking out. Luckily at that point my friends came in and they saw it and it just vanished."

Her friends later told her they saw a dark shadow in there with her that disappeared when they entered. Years removed from it now, she still cannot decide who won that night. "I think it was a draw. It really scared me, like what the hell was I doing there, but I proved it was there."

The evil in the tower might have a memory. She feels years later she saw the eyes following her while she walked outside long after the confrontation. It watched her walk by as another witness saw the eyes focus on her.

Lillie knows what she saw and fought with what was more than an urban legend. "I'm not sure what was up there. After that night, I never parked in the front and never went near the chapel for the rest of the year. There was a dirt road that went into the back. I always went out back and parked near the back door of the wing where my friends were living. I haven't been up on campus for some time. It was not a pleasant feeling. It was very scary."

Part Six

Ghostly Cities,
Places, & Objects

The Haunted City

Extending just past Coleman's established Triangle is the city of Newport, Rhode Island. If we follow the stories and reports, the Triangle extends into New Bedford, Fairhaven, and Acushnet, so why stop because of a manmade border. There are parts of Rhode Island experiencing the same kind of activity seen in other parts of the Triangle, and energy does not recognize state lines. Several towns in Rhode Island used to be part of Freetown, so why should the curse of the Triangle not follow the land over.

Newport has long been considered one of the most haunted cities in New England, and with so much history there are plenty of stories as to who the ghosts may be. The city has seen its share of bad times and abuses during the good times, creating a unique mix of emotions and an excellent setting for a good ghost story. While most cities have had ghost tours as a quiet attraction for years, Newport has been vocal about the spirits there for decades and has made it a business drawing those in looking to hear the tales.

It all starts with the houses that draw the tourists. The mansions on the coast of Newport are a testament to affluence in New England. They stand as a reminder of how the other half live, and mansion after mansion boasts plush lawns, intricate stonework, and a great view. They are also some of the most haunted buildings in America.

Bellevue Avenue in Newport is like a paranormal circuit into the world of the unknown with quick access to haunted Ocean Drive and the Cliff Walk. The mansions, most of which are open to tours, can all be reached by this main road. Visitors can go and explore without a plan or take some time to sort things out ahead of time. Either way, legends and hauntings mix, and anyone interested in ghosts could spend a weekend there without hearing the same story twice.

The crowning jewel of the area may be Belcourt Castle, which boasts a phantom monk and a haunted suit of armor. Brenton Point is a once brilliant palace thought to be cursed because of Egyptian artifacts taken out of the Valley of the Kings by one of its owners. Visitors can visit the Astors Beechwood Mansion where the ghost of a former maid haunts the halls trying to work out her own suicide.

If travelers to Newport do not wish to take a break from the paranormal, they can stay at any number of haunted inns and eat at one of several restaurants with a history of apparitions. One of the most popular is the Black Duck Inn. According to Thomas D'Agostino in his book, *Haunted Rhode Island*, the bed and breakfast was originally a rum house during Prohibition that was raided by the coast guard. Three people were killed, which sparked off a clash between the soldiers and the townspeople. Ghosts in the building have been known to turn lights and radios on and off and lock and unlock deadbolts. Voices and footsteps have been heard.

Whispers have been heard about another site in Newport, and besides the geography, this one has a tighter connection to the Bridgewater Triangle. While it was still an active quarry, the stones taken out of the Assonet Ledge were used for buildings in the area, including Taunton State Hospital, several of the estates on the water in Newport, and Fort Adams, an inactive military base in Newport dating back to the Revolutionary War when the original groundwork was laid down for what would be a fully operational stone fortress.

Fort Adams has never seen military action, but the soldiers who once called it home have fought for this country since its beginning. Designed to protect the city and not allow the enemy a foothold in New England with access to Boston, the garrison is now an empty shell. It no longer houses soldiers, but the memories of what it once was remain in the minds of those who walk through. It is in a state of disrepair, preserved but still rundown in sections, and leaving the tour group you come in with may lead to getting lost for a few hours.

This is New England, and preservation is an industry, so people are welcome to come and see the old fort for themselves. They can tour the upper ridges where soldiers once stood guard and walk the rooms they stayed in, being careful not to snag their clothes on nails and boards. The most exciting attraction is the underground tunnels. No more than six feet tall and underneath the entire property inside the wall, the tunnels are a damp and dark reminder of military conditions of the past. Tourists are given flashlights and asked to point them at the shoes of the people in front of them for light. When you finish, you get an official "Tunnel Rat" bumper sticker.

There is another tour that draws people in, but this one is only done for a month every year. In October, the place becomes known as the Fortress of Nightmares, and Robert J. McCormack, director of Visitor Services, helps people to understand the haunted history of Newport and some of the scarier stories associated with the structure. The tour is a tribute to New England storytelling, half-truth and half legend, but its success has forced people to ask if Fort Adams is indeed haunted.

McCormack answers the questions very carefully. "Any publicity gets people to come and visit, so I'll let the rumors persist, but when push comes to shove, I have to say there are no ghosts." In addition to having never seen a ghost there himself, he has never heard of anyone ever reporting a specter. "I've never personally seen a ghost and I'd be pretty surprised if there was one. If anything, there might be a large raccoon." Instead, he attributes any rumors to the age of the building and the imagination the creepiness inspires....

"It's a big old scary place that's been around with so much history attached to it. It must have something."

There are stories though, and people have seen things they cannot explain while touring. Fort Adams is more than just a good setting for a haunting. It is a place KNOWN to be haunted.

The most haunted place may be the tunnels. While they are a fun place to explore and get scared in on most days, others have had unexplained experiences. There might be a good reason for this. "There were a few construction issues with the tunnels that collapsed and walls that didn't hold," says McCormack. "There are records of a few workers who were killed. People

The passageway where people have seen unexplained shadows and lights.

go down into the tunnels and think they feel a breeze, but there's air ventilation down there. Otherwise it's probably the claustrophobia factor. It can be a little creepy."

Despite having a reason not to be haunted, some have lived through things they cannot explain. Joss is not claustrophobic or afraid of the dark, but he knows he touched a ghost in the tunnels, or at least that a ghost touched him.

"I was the last in line. Okay, I was the last in line because I was lagging behind, trying to find little hidden things in the tunnels. I was maybe ten feet from the next person in front of me. I felt a hand on my shoulder. Not a feeling like the wind or something, but a touch and then pressure, like someone was forcing down on me and tightening their grip."

The sensation made him jump, forcing him to hit his shoulder and neck on the roof of the tunnel. He turned around as quickly as he could, but there was no one there. "I could feel cold breath on me. Then my flashlight dimmed, turned off, and turned back on brighter than before."

Carol had something similar happen to her. "I was in the tunnels and heard my name being called inside my head. It was a man's voice, definitely not mine, and he was whispering. Then I felt hands on my waist. There was no one around me. The next person was at least three feet away. Maybe it was just my imagination, but it tried to pick me up."

There are other candidates for haunted location at the fort. It always had a somewhat strained relationship with the town it protected. Soldiers were known to go into the city and make trouble or have local disputes end in violence. There was once a riot in town involving troops from Fort Adams and at least one soldier died.

Then there was the long march home. "The whole harbor would freeze over and you could walk from the local bar downtown back over to Fort Adams," claims McCormack. "There are a number who tried it a little later in the season than they should have. There are a few who fell through the ice." Many who fell through were captured by local icon Ida Lewis, but a few died in the water. Their bodies are buried in a cemetery on the property, along with a few who died during a polio epidemic in early 1900s.

These deaths might explain the figures seen on the stairs leading up to the top of the fort. Several people have reported seeing a man dressed in military clothes who walked with haste up them and who disappears before he reaches the top. Others have seen a similarly dressed man who walked the top, as if on guard duty, who also vanished. One such sighting happened near the burnt out second floor.

In the beginning of the twentieth century, the large cannons were removed and renovations took place, including the building of a second floor in part of the fortress. There was a fire in 1947, but no one died. The event was enough to spark rumors of soldiers burning and coming back to haunt the area.

Sally never saw those ghosts, but she saw a man trying to get back to Fort Adams. "It was too far away. I couldn't see his face or clothes in detail, but he was floating on the water, like walking. I knew he was a soldier because he was wearing a uniform and had a hat on. He was also walking in that way soldiers do, even when they are off duty." Sally says she turned to point him out to her friend and he was gone.

There is something more like a shadow seen by people on the tour. As the guide talks, people are encouraged to walk through what used to be rooms and stations, some with places to point a gun out of. The areas are now cramped with broken boards and exposed foundations. At the right angle, someone can look through several of these rooms at once. Several people have reported seeing something dark, too large to be raccoons, darting in the next room. When they check, nothing is there.

Fort Adams has housed Presidents and other important people for over two hundred years. Although it has never been the site of a battle, it has seen its share of trainings and exercises. It holds a small part of our past, standing tall as a witness to the forming and growth of a great nation. There is something there that continues to watch the present become the past, and like a soldier on watch, these spirits never rest.

The Summer Vacation

This story was originally posted on Ghostvillage at www.ghostvillage.com and used with permission by the author and the site's administrator, Jeff Belanger.

Sharon is a naturally sensitive person who now spends her time investigating the paranormal. She is considered an authority on demons and considers herself a demon hunter, visiting haunted houses and separating ghosts from their stronger, shadowy counterparts. She has experienced several different types of unexplained creatures and forces and has the skills and abilities to handle most anything she comes into contact with. Things were not always that way. Living at the very edge of the Bridgewater Triangle, she credits starting her journey into the paranormal with something she experienced in 1984 when she was only fifteen.

It all started when she first went into a rental home and had a psychic experience. "My family saved for months to rent a vacation home on Cape Cod. It was in the little village of Wareham near Onset, and the whole area was made up of vacation homes. When we got there, I was excited and immediately ran into the house only to run through a wall of cold. The cold "got in" and took over my mind. I was pushed to the back of my mind and this other being thought through me and touched things with my body."

Although only a teenager, she had already had several experiences with ghosts and the darker elements, but nothing like she was experiencing in the house. In a way, whatever was there had already begun taking control of her and was pressing its will into hers. It had the ability to control her thoughts, and as suddenly as it came to her, it spoke in plain terms, as if they had been friends. While what the spirit was saying was not alarming, the loss of control became too much. Whatever it was had her mind and her body.

"The entity actually held a conversation with me about what she remembered things being like in her day. The strangest part of this was that my vision changed. I wear glasses, but she took them off. Also, all colors paled into a weird black and white vision. I was terrified. No matter how I squirmed I could not break loose."

Having no training on how to deal with something this intense and not knowing what was happening to her, she could do nothing but hear what she was being told. The spirit, who she felt as a female presence, had complete control of her, and although she could see what was happening to her, she could not move at will or break free.

"My mother called me outside, and as she went to see who my mother was, my body crossed the threshold of the door and the entity was popped out. I was panicked, but what could I do? Saying nothing, I built a wall up in my head that said simply, 'No.' My little brother and sister [had gone] upstairs, soon came down screaming that a dead hand had reached in to the open window. I had not told anyone about my encounter, but my, 'No' strategy was working. I cradled them in my arms and said, 'No,' to the ghost for them as well."

The possession subsided, but the paranormal activity continued as the family tried to settle in and enjoy their vacation. "We had so much poltergeist activity in that house! Like the salt and peppershakers would fly off the fridge and onto the table. My Mom would put things away, turn around, and they would be back. We also experienced knocks, footsteps, and bad smells. And when my cousin came to visit, he stuck his head through the open window that led from the TV room to the porch, a window that was so jammed all three of us could not budge it, and it slammed down on his head." There were also the cold spots Sharon would feel and an unexplained sour odor that followed her in the house. Even when nothing was happening, there was still something dark in the house Sharon could feel. She was the only one who had the instincts to react. "My baby sister was stationed in a crib in my room. She often woke up around 2 or 3 a.m. screaming. I got good at waking up when the presence got near and throwing my protective, 'No' over the baby too."

Answers came after the fact. "At the end of the week I finally told my Mom about the encounter I had. She believed me and went to see the realtor we had leased the house from. He casually told us that the reason we got the house so cheap was because it was haunted. A woman had been murdered there twenty years ago."

That did not stop her family from coming back to the house to stay for other vacations. With the reason for the spirit known, it was easier for the family to deal with the moving objects and the weird sounds. Her mother even felt bad about the hauntings because they pointed at the tragedy that had happened there.

"We rented that house out a couple more times. Since we knew it was haunted, we would say hello to the ghost (my Mom felt bad for her) when we got there. It was never easy for me, as she often tried to get into my head, or talk to me."

The entire experience was negative for Sharon, mainly due to the intrusive and overpowering nature of it, but the lessons learned in the house helped her later on in life. "I built up my Auric protection from that experience, but I was very afraid of ghosts for a long time afterwards. As will happen, ghosts were very interested in me. Then demons started being put in my path. It is one thing to believe in ghosts, but it took much convincing and hand-wringing to accept that there are demons."

In the Bridgewater Triangle, the wolves come in sheep clothing and the lines between the two are easily blurred.

The Haunted Violin

Not all of the oddities of the Triangle are natural. The energy that attracts the odd, the unexplained cult activity, and the weird beasts also encourages other things to come within its lines. Some might say things in the Triangle are haunted and some might say the area changes things, including people's perceptions. Haunted living comes with the territory, and much like an old New England curse, that does not always limit itself to things we can see or noises we cannot explain. Sometimes an object can be touched by the paranormal, and in Southeastern Massachusetts, the paranormal is sometimes imported.

According to two separate sources, one such import was capable of making beautiful music or waking up the dead. In 1945 a local musician, teacher, and musical repairman from Wareham bought a Hornsteiner violin that is rumored to have been built in Germany sometime in the late eighteenth century. For Harold Cudworth the purchase was about a passion for collecting old instruments, and despite its beauty and history and his own love of the instrument, the violin was one of dozens of antiques he owned in his vast collection. The violin, however, carried more than just the tradition of European craftsmanship.

Shortly after buying the instrument, Cudworth began playing "The Broken Melody" by Van Biene. In *Ghostly Haunts* by locally renowned folklorist and author Robert Ellis Cahill, the musician recalls a disturbing noise coming from the kitchen, much like a broken sink would make. It stopped when he stopped playing and he chalked it up to coincidence until he played the same tune a few weeks later while practicing for a concert.

Again the noise came, although this time it originated from above him, and again it started and stopped with his playing. He tried to exhaust any logical explanation for the noise, and came up empty. He played the Hornsteiner several more times, and with each playing he avoided the song. He eventually thought everything was in his head, and not being a superstitious man, played the song. He finished, went back to some repair work he was doing, and was disturbed a few minutes later by the latch on his door rattling. The door was shut, but as he began down the stairs he heard the same door slam behind him. He looked, but the door was still open.

This continued several more times. He was never scared by what happened, just curious as to why his instrument and why that song. His work took him to different locations within the Triangle, including a home in New Bedford where he taught lessons to a young girl. He played the song for the girl's father and the front door of the house began to open and close violently for no reason. In Rochester he played the tune for a woman who asked him to stop because she was feeling "funny." In Massapoisett his playing caused the pictures on the wall to rock back and forth, but not before pausing once it reached apex each time.

Cudworth eventually retired the instrument, because he found one he liked more and not because of the shake it caused. There is no record of the violin before it came into his hands, although certain details link it to royalty in Europe, and there is no record of the disturbances ever happening outside of the Triangle. The cursed object never had issues with other songs, and the tune caused no trouble when played on any other instrument. All we are left with is a story of a man, his instrument, and a lonely song that touched the *other side.*

Friends and Bunnies

The Triangle does draw negative energy into it, but it also has an odd effect on the people who live there. Sometimes it can make the worst come out in people, causing normal events to sour quickly or making people do things they would not normally do. Friends become enemies without explanation. It usually goes unnoticed until there is some kind of paranormal activity involved. Then the person searches websites and local media for some answers and finds information about the Bridgewater Triangle. The small moments where people stepped outside of themselves and became people they were not make sense only in retrospect and in context.

Amy enjoyed living with her friends. She, her husband, and their daughter lived in a rented house with another couple and their daughter on South Main Street in Attleboro. The arrangement worked out well. The rent and bills were split, and Amy stayed home taking care of both girls. It might have been a good situation financially, but soon after moving in, she did not like staying in the house alone for long hours. There was something else in there with her and the girls, and it started to get worse in the early part of the summer.

"I just had this feeling about it. I don't know what it was, but it was creepy. A few months go by and I started noticing things." Amy says she would often shut off a light and come back a time later and it would be on again. This often happened when she was alone and the girls were in another part of the house. She would frequently wake up in the middle of the night, roused out of a deep sleep. She would not see or hear anything, and the room would be eerily still, but she would wonder what had woken her up.

It started to become too much for her. The house had gone from pleasant to unnerving to scary in the space of a few months. "I would have this feeling I couldn't explain. I'd make my husband get up with me in the middle of the night to take me to the bathroom because I was that scared. I know he started to feel the same way because he started waking me up in the night to go with him to the bathroom."

Whatever it was finally made itself known near Christmas. "I was sitting on the living room floor watching TV. From the corner of my eye I saw this black shadow race across the floor right next to me. I jumped and yelled. I thought it was a rat or something, but we looked everywhere in the living room and found nothing." With no natural explanation for what she had seen, she started to put the other pieces together. She began to believe the house was haunted, and the negative feeling she was getting forced her to face the fact it might be something that did not like the couples.

Things started to change in the house. She and her husband were not sleeping well at night and would become quick with each other. For some reason, the tension spread to the couple they lived with, but there was something deeper than arguments about nothing or misunderstandings. "My husband started to fight with our other roommate who had been his friend for ten years. I started fighting with his friend's wife and him. My husband started thinking I was having an affair with his friend. All this crazy stuff and all this fighting and arguing didn't make sense. We were all good friends for years until we moved into this house."

Anyone who has moved in with a friend knows these things happen. It is one thing to like a person and be close, but it is quite another to have to look at them everyday and have their little habits and rituals directly affect you. This was beyond hairs in the sink and unwashed dishes however. The couple began having violent thoughts about each other and the irrational allegations continued. Eventually the couple moved out.

That did not stop the activity in the house. "A few days later me and my daughter were sitting on my bed and I was looking at a book. Again from the corner of my eye, I see this black shadow moving slowly along the floor. I didn't pay any mind. I thought it was our cat. I could see the shadow moving towards the toy box. Right then my daughter jumped and screamed. I jumped because whatever that shadow was it was not the cat. I grabbed my daughter and walked towards the toy box and looked around. There was nothing there. I ran so fast out of that room and started screaming for my husband. I told him what happened and then my daughter said, 'Yea, Papa. It was a bunny with no eyes.' That night we all slept in the bed together and I remember holding my necklace that had a cross on it and praying.

It is unclear just what was in the house, but the family moved out shortly after. Things settled down for them, but they never talked to the other family or found out if they had anything happen to them. The emotional manipulation, the description of the bunny, and the dark figure in the house suggests it might have been demonic in nature. The community was referred to as the Old Mill Houses, which might point to the land's use as mill property. There may have been negative energy left there from some tragedy at the business from long ago, and a spirit might have been lying dormant, waiting for a trigger to get energy from. The analysis means little to Amy. All she knows is she lost her mind, her friends, and a great house. Touching the *other side* sometimes means leaving things behind.

In the Bedroom

Jason is an eighteen-year-old son of Portuguese immigrants who have lived in the Fall River and New Bedford area since their arrival in America twenty years ago. Members of his family have been experiencing the paranormal for decades, first in Portugal and then in the Triangle. For the older generation it is something common, but not to be talked about. When brought up, his mother might recall a time in Lisbon when she was kidnapped by a gang of teens and held for ransom and kept company by the ghost of a little girl. She dismisses the kidnapping and instead still talks about her phantom friend in glowing terms, but she rarely talks about it at all.

Jason grew up in this world. He knew there was something *other* than this world, but wasn't allowed to reveal the small things he was living through. They did not really disturb him. He was entertained by seeing what other people could not, and in some ways, at least early on, it was like a game. There was something wrong in the house on South Main Street in Fall River though, and what was once a special gift became a nightmare for the little ten-year-old boy who could see spirits.

The landlord told them the three-bedroom apartment had a history of weird things happening, but he would not get into it any further. Instead he passed Jason's parents a knowing look, and they decided it was worth it. The rent was much cheaper than where they were staying, and Jason's father, who worked two jobs and drove a Sunday paper route, was more down to earth than his wife. He was not going to let a great apartment closer to work go because of some Old World superstitions. Perhaps he also knew he would not be spending too much time in the house anyway.

They soon moved in and got to know the other families in the house. They had seen ghosts and were willing to share everything they knew. Today Jason cannot remember many of the stories, but the basic ideas and how he felt about them have remained.

They shared their stories with Jason and his mother as if they were happening to someone else and somehow added to the feeling of dread. "They were like ghosts stories to me. I never took them as a warning, and I couldn't tell what my mom thought. She just let me listen. A little kid."

There had been reports from other people living in the apartment of shining figures walking the stairs and forming in bedrooms. Things were found moved and there were sometimes noises coming from the kitchens when no one was in there. People heard them in their own apartments, but they became more afraid when they heard them in other people's homes. They knew them to be empty, and they would sit with all the lights on hoping they would stay away from their bedrooms.

For the first four months nothing unusual happened, and the whole family ignored the cold spots occurring randomly throughout the house. "It was summer, and sometimes you'd have to wear a coat in the kitchen." He and his family were never sure what rooms would get cold or for how long. It just became part of their routine, and they walked around the house with sweatshirts tied around their waists just in case.

It was Jason's room that became the source of tension in the house. One night, around 1 a.m., he got up to go to the bathroom. When he returned to the room the window was open. He did not remember opening it, but shut it and returned to bed. He tried to go back to sleep, but he opened his eyes again when he heard his window slowly opening again. He raised his head, but there was no one else in the room.

"I was too lazy to get up and close it, so I tried to forget it and went back to sleep." Instead he kept thinking about the window until finally he started to doze off. As soon as he put his head back down, the window slammed shut. He sat up and watched as the window opened and closed four or five times while he watched. He ran out and slept on the couch.

Over the next few days he begged his parents not to make him stay in the room and they eventually broke down and moved his little sister in there. After a few nights she experienced the same thing and "flipped out."

The family refused to move her. Jason remembers sleeping in the next room listening to his sister weep. "I could've been braver, but I was scared. I wasn't going back in there."

The family moved out less than a month later, and until he was older, no one ever told him why.

"It was my sister. She asked me a while ago if I remembered the house. I said I didn't remember anything except it being cold and my window opening. She told me she had woken up one night because the window kept closing. She had opened it a few times, but then it would slam shut. Finally, she opened it and put a book there. Ten minutes later she heard the book crash on the floor. She hid under the sheets, but felt the room get real cold. She finally came out, and when she did, there was an old woman dressed in a long white dress. The woman looked her straight in the eye, shook her head like she was angry, and shut the window."

The Man in the Window

There is another classic story that exists as a companion to the hitchhiker urban legend. In this myth a man goes to his front door to find a frantic priest. The man, far from being a religious person, allows him in and offers some tea to settle his nerves. The priest says he cannot because he needs to see the sick woman who called him. He had just seen a mysterious woman at a nearby restaurant telling him to come to the address to give a dying woman her last rights. The man says he lives alone, and there is no one there close to death. The priest, looking over the man's shoulder, sees a picture of the man's dead mother. "That is the woman I saw," he says. The man breaks down crying because his mother had passed quickly and was not able to receive the sacrament before her demise. The priest does a makeshift blessing postmortem and the man turns his life around and finds Jesus.

It is the kind of story that makes the hairs on our neck rise and makes us nod our heads because of the sheer truthfulness of it even though we know it is not true. In the Triangle, urban legends often come to life. They say all myths have a hint of truth, but in Southeastern Massachusetts, the difference is the stories are told in the first person. The legend is a ghost story and not a fable.

Dave's house on Sycamore Street in Fairhaven was haunted for the entire time he lived there. Although he was very young, he remembers furniture would move by itself in the house. He was not sure what to think of it all. Too young to be really scared and too old to ignore it all, he was more confused and curious, until what was in the house reached out to the outside world.

One day he was playing outside his house when a cab from New Bedford pulled up. The cab driver blew the horn and asked Dave to let the "old man" know he was there. It was a strange request because it was only he and his parents living in the house and no older man had been there for quite some time. His mother came to his side to see what was going on, and the driver grew more impatient. Dave asked what old man.

"The driver motioned to the front right parlor window. 'That old man,' he said. My mom and I turned and looked into the living room front window. The image of an old man was in the window. I looked at my mom and she looked at me. We both witnessed or saw this individual in the window looking out and then this old man disappeared, dissolved." Dave describes the man as wearing a button up brown sweater. He also claims he was short and looked like he was from the old country. He remembers thinking it might have been his grandfather who had passed away, but his mother told him years later it could not have been him.

Dave, his mother, and the man in the car all saw the man in the window. "The cab driver took off in a hurry. I never saw that cab again." The driver's reaction tells him he must have seen the man disappear before his eyes.

The family moved from the house less than a year later and he never saw the ghost again. He never found out who the man was or if he was responsible for the moving furniture and other weird things that happened in the house. According to Dave, who still lives in the area, the house has been sold numerous times since his family moved out. No one stays there for too long. Maybe they stay just long enough to meet the ghost who wants to leave the house.

Don't Look Too Much

*"I believe if you want something to happen, it will happen.
If you go looking for something, you'll find it."*

Dee firmly believes this, but for her it is more than just a philosophy of life or a religious ideal. When a ghost appears in a house, most people want it to go away. There may be an interest in why the ghost is there, but an intruder is an intruder and the uninvited guest cannot leave too soon. Others consciously invite the spirits in, looking for some answers or insight. Dee didn't mind thinking her house was haunted at first, but when she realized she had allowed it in and the nature of the hauntings intensified, she changed her life in hopes that she could remove it.

Dee's parents' house in Attleboro, Massachusetts, was not always haunted. She lived there almost her whole life and the family had been the first to inhabit it. There were no reports of ancient Indian burial grounds or abandoned cemeteries beneath its foundation or any activity to suggest it. Pictures never showed orbs or odd streaks of light, and there were no unexplained noises or cold spots that would raise an eye. All that could be said was that Dee had a normal and healthy interest in ghosts stories and horror movies.

After exploring some local legends and haunted places, Dee became a ghost hunter. She would traverse the graveyards of nearby towns and take pictures to analyze. She watched the shows and documentaries on television and learned the lingo. She lived in the Bridgewater Triangle, and haunted locations were never hard to find. She had been hearing stories since she was a child, and with the renewed interest, more people were coming forward with their stories of local hauntings. She would go out almost every weekend looking for evidence of life after death, and at one point her interest drew in her father. They would often go on investigations together and travel to other haunted places to gather more information.

Shortly after her father started to go out with her, she noticed a difference in her parent's house. She had moved in while attending graduate school, but something had changed. "Sometimes at night I would feel a presence in my room. Something was in there with me. I would have to sleep with the TV on or the lava lamp." She began to get an eerie feeling and at times, especially at night and alone in her room, she would feel on edge and could not relax. It was not every night, but it began to be frequent enough to upset her.

She shared her concern with her father, who believed her. He began taking random pictures of the house, mostly of Dee and began to get unexplained flashes of light and weird figures in the shots. She was still going out looking for ghosts, and she had not seen or heard anything, so she was able to brush off most of what was happening. For her, there was never a connection between what was going on in her house and her increasingly obsessive search for evidence.

Whatever was in the house was just getting started. "My parents do a lot of camping so they would go away for the weekend. One weekend I was home there with my grandmother." Dee explains she was sitting in a chair facing the television that stands between two large windows and talking on the phone. "I was looking at the left window. I could see the reflection of my grandmother watching TV. Just beyond her right in the hallway, there was the silhouette of a man. Standing there. As I'm looking at it, he turned his head and walked towards the kitchen."

She describes the man she saw as looking much like the shadow people or dark men seen in other places throughout the Triangle. They are a common occurrence in the world of the paranormal and are different in many ways from traditional ghosts. They are generally found in places where there is other activity and are believed to feed off the energy these other ghosts might produce. The sighting happened quickly and Dee was most confused by the absence of sound during it.

Although she was not entirely scared by the incident, she wanted an explanation of what was going on. Feeling uneasy was one thing. She tried to deny what she had seen. "You have to convince yourself you didn't see something, but you did." She consulted some people she had been sharing evidence with and was told by one of them to talk to the spirits and see if there was anything she could do for them. "One day I was home alone. I was talking to them, taking some pictures of the living room." When she developed them later she found two figures staring back at her. One was the man she had seen going into the kitchen. The other was a woman, although the photo was grainy and could have been another man with long hair and possibly a beard.

She began to question what she was doing in her spare time. Like many investigators, something was coming home with her or finding its way back to her. Many believe looking for ghosts leaves a person open. Spirits wanting to make contact and finding most people looking the other way see these people like a beacon and flock to them to try and make contact. This in turn can also allow the darker, more sinister things to find the person, like a predator finding a water supply to feed off the smaller animals drinking.

One night Dee and her friend were watching a movie in the living room. Her parents were again camping and she had invited her over because she did not feel comfortable in the house by herself anymore. Her dog was lying on the floor near them when it suddenly got up. It went to the stairs, looked up to the second floor, and began whimpering. Dee looked over as it began to back up into the room.

She still finds it hard to describe exactly what she saw. The figure on the stairs looked like a distortion, like it bent the light around it to hide it, or like the heat rising from pavement on a hot day. This is another type of ghost seen often around the Triangle. It has been seen, among other places, near an old foundation behind the Freetown State Forest associated with an old woman who haunted several young boys in the area and the Holy Cross Chapel at Stonehill College. Actually what it might be is not yet known, but it implies a break in dimensions or a pulse of energy not strong enough to take form. In religious terms, it might be a spirit in limbo and not have enough consciousness to retake its old form.

"I could only see parts of its outline. Not a full outline but you could see some sort of mass coming down the stairs." Dee was about fifteen feet away, but her friend was closer, with her back to it. "It got to the bottom of the stairs between the stairs and the front door and I was just looking at it. I was terrified. I was completely concentrated on it and I just kind of froze. It just kind of dissipated."

Almost instantly, she knew what she had seen was different from the thing she had been seeing out of the corner of her eye or through the mirror. "Right at that time I felt like someone took a bucket of water and poured it over my head. I felt it go all the way down to my toes." Her friend could sense something was wrong, but Dee had not broken out of her trance yet. "Right at that same moment she felt someone squeezed all the air out of her lungs like when you are on a rollercoaster."

That had been the last straw. She began to avoid cemeteries and all but stopped investigating. "I made myself lose interest." Things had gone too far and she felt the reward of getting something in the field was not worth the intensifying evidence she was seeing with her own two eyes at home. The activity slowed and then stopped. Things went back to normal in her childhood home and the feelings in her bedroom went away. Months later her father shared something with her he had been silent about so he would not scare her. He had seen a ghost in the same area twice in the past few months. "Out of the corner of his eye he saw a man in a brown trenchcoat standing at the foot of the stairs." The man was much clearer than the things she had seen.

Although it was intense at the time, Dee still wonders about the ghosts she saw in the house. The living room and front stairs seemed to have the most activity, which would make sense given the layout of her house. The stairs lead to the front door, an extremely common area for ghosts to enter and exit a house, and the living room feeds off that entrance as well. She is still torn over how to feel about them. "I never felt threatened. I just felt creepy, especially when I was alone."

She has started going back out to look for ghosts in cemeteries and known haunted places, and hopes they do not follow her home. For her, the setting for a good horror story is best when she does not have to sleep there.

Part Seven

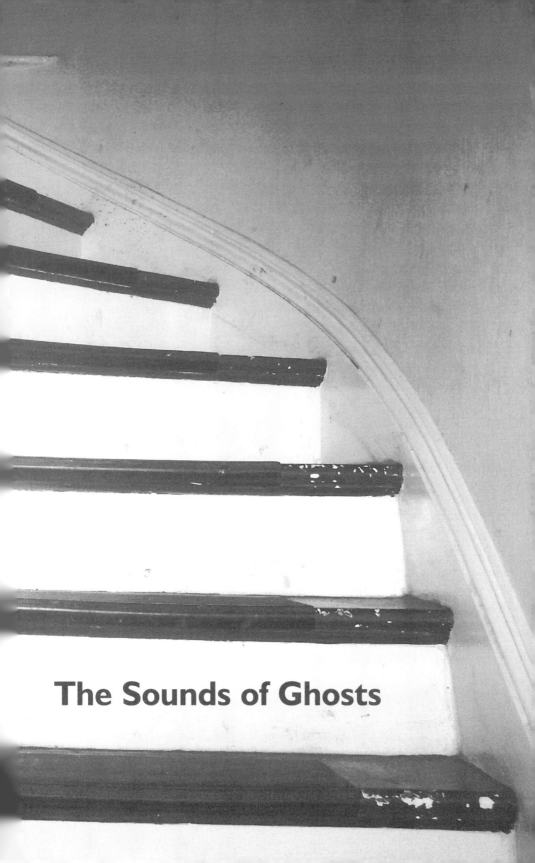

The Sounds of Ghosts

The EVP Guy

M ike Markowicz does not see ghosts—and he does not care to. It is an unusual perspective from a man who spends a great deal of his time searching for ghosts, but Mike is anything but usual in the paranormal community. Mike is a techie, a lover of the technology behind investigating, and spends his free time bent over evidence and trying to perfect the tools of his trade. He has spent more than five thousand dollars and hundreds of hours honing his skills, but he does not care about the things he sees or the images on a two dimensional photo.

Mike is an EVP guy, but that only touches the surface of what he does. EVP stands for Electronic Voice Phenomenon and what he is doing is trying to capture the voices of the dead. Spirit communication is the next step in the paranormal movement, and he is one of the forerunners in developing the machines that will open up a new world.

He first began his work four years ago. He was a fan of paranormal shows and loved a good ghost story, but there was always something sterile about them for him. One Halloween night a friend showed him an EVP she had received in a haunted house. While two women carried on a conversation about place settings, a third woman, unseen, screamed. "That's it. I was hooked." He went out and bought a cheap handheld digital recorder and began trying to catch the voices of the dead. He eventually invested in a better recorder and the number of voices he heard went up.

"When you're alone in a room and you get something, and you know you're all alone, what else could it be? It is the energy of someone in the room that's not. It could just be psychic spillage and its going somewhere and spilling over into this world. I began to think, 'If I got a better recorder and the number went up, what if I got better microphones. Imagine what I could get.'"

Over the next four years he continued to experiment with different ways of recording and capturing sound. He now has ten high quality microphones that he brings to an investigation and which he sets up more like a rock concert than a ghost hunt. He runs all the equipment through a mixing board to control sound levels and then a transmitter that converts what is recorded into digital information. The whole thing runs into his computer where it is recorded and can then be cleaned up and played back. The set up is much more complex than most people who do what he does, but he believes it is needed to advance the field and get the best results.

"You can hear the house breathe."

Tinnitus in both of his ears has limited his normal hearing. Rock concerts and firing guns without protection caused a permanent ringing that affects his normal life. He believes it has helped him become a better listener for EVPs. "Just like everything, the more you practice, the better you get. I have listened to thousands of hours of these recordings, and I think it has made me develop a better ear for them. I think I have actually changed the synopsis in my brain. I hear things other people don't."

Current technology is limited, and Mike began his quest to develop new devices. He has converted speakers into microphones and manipulated recording devices to try and get stronger evidence. "I wanted to see how a microphone works. Why didn't they go from 1 hertz to above 20,000? I did some research on the Internet and found this guy trying to build a two-way communication device. This was just what I wanted." The two eventually shared information and Mike began using the man's design to develop his own Spiritcom, a device intended to carry on a two-way communication with the *other side*. Although much of the design is still a secret, Mike says he used it the first time and received a person singing "Amazing Grace"—something that helped to change the way he thinks about investigating.

He then got in touch with Frank Sumption who was working on what has now been dubbed, Frank's Box. Frank was running microphone and recording devices through empty computer shells and then manually scanning radio stations. The basic idea behind the box is that radio signals create energy for the spirits to use, and the use of the box continues to be a source of controversy and tension among investigators. Mike used the basic theory to create a device he laughingly calls 'Mike's Tube.' He took piping and attached it to a short wave radio. The results were quick and, in his opinion, revolutionary.

"There have been a lot of people who have come up with devices, and they all work. The very first communication devices started to have EVPs. I think it is a combination of technology and intent. If you don't want to pick up anything, it's not going to work."

If that was the end of Mike's story, he would be like many EVP specialists across the country, but Mike is unique among his peers. Most organized paranormal groups have a person who is responsible for the technology of the investigation. While all members understand why things work the way they do and have a basic handle on the science, the tech manager is the straight man. He is usually the no-nonsense, black and white person of the team; very rarely does he mention the word soul, and when he says the word "spirit," he is referring to a ghost. They almost never talk to God.

The EVP guy sees things a different way. "It's completely spiritual." Acoustic energy is limited, and unlike most people who work with EVPs, Mike does not believe that is what is being recorded. Instead, it is the sound of the soul, or spiritual energy, that converts itself to an audio wave we can hear. The voices are connected to God. For him the soul of a man is theorized next to string theory and the idea of relativity. Science and religion often conflict, but not for Mike—especially when he's sitting in front of his mixing board and computer.

Early on in life he was exposed to something not of this world. While mowing the lawn as a teen, he felt his third eye – the psychic side of one's self and the gateway to revelation in some cultures – open up. It was only for a moment, but in that time he saw his aunt and uncle pull up to the house and the winning number in that night's lottery. His relatives unexpectedly arrived from Canada later that day and the number came out. With that small revelation, his spiritual journey began, but it was not until he was exposed to the world of spirit communication things made sense. "I hear EVPs a little differently than other people. I got someone once who said, 'I will talk to you tonight.'" Mike did not evaluate the evidence until later that night, when he realized the spirit was indeed talking to him "tonight." It seems simple, but it changed the way he approached the paranormal. He feels more like the spirit had followed him home, and the person's voice on tape seemed to get stronger. "I shut everything off, but I could still hear the voice. I could hear the talking and this electronic popping. It was at that point my hearing turned on. If I could hear them with my naked ear, it can't be anything else other than spiritual energy.

"It's not just science. If you have something awful happen to you and you scream very loudly and you die. You might be trapped there because something traumatic happened. The memory that you have is one of acoustical energy. In your memory you have the memory of the sound. If you want to communicate that to someone, it's not going to be an acoustical wave anymore. It's going to be in a spiritual wave form."

Mike feels he now has the ability to hear spirits without equipment, but he also has the ability to hear himself. "I can read from a book and hear it in my ear. If I don't think about it, I can hear my subconscious." This fits in with another of his deviations from the EVP norm. Mike believes the thoughts, emotions, and energy of the living can be transferred while trying to communicate with a ghost. "I think they come from living people because we share the same energy as the spirit does."

Voices on tape are not just the random gathering of information, but also a message from another world meant to be heard and learned from. The spiritual world is one of melody and rhythm. There is something about our human experience that interferes with a universal song being created and so we lose our connection to the music. Spirits, who now only exist as spiritual energy, are more in touch with this. Most of the EVPs he has collected have a similar rhythm to the speech. They communicate almost in a singsong way. "Even the angry ones. I have EVPs I collected in Hull and the guy is swearing at me in song." He feels this is because all spirits, regardless of their evolution, can hear the songs sung by God more than those left behind.

The dead all become part of the song. The reason we do not hear people who have passed is because we are not set up to. "They want their voices to be heard. We don't hear it because our ears are designed to pick up an acoustic wave, not a spiritual one. Just like our ears don't pick up a microwave or a radio wave."

In several locations in the Triangle, including the Hockomock Swamp, he has received recordings of people singing. The music they create is beautiful and in complete harmony and points to something larger. "The more you understand, the more glory you have. From the outside looking in, you don't have that much. The closer you are the more you'll see. It's all a song in praise of God. You're on the outside. You know it's there, but you can't reach it. It's a tough place to be. It's the basis of all that you are in that form. It could raise you up, and you can't have it. Just knowing it you would be in a hallowed place next to God. That song is a constant song, and you became part of the whole. It's like a jigsaw puzzle and it goes on forever. Each jigsaw piece is a person, and together it makes up the outer light that is the beginning of heaven. The more elevated you become. You're in the presence of God."

Spirit communication is the way for us to see these glimpses of heaven, and perhaps make the transit of our own death easier. "The person who discovers the energy of the human soul is going to create the perfect communication device. It's going to open everything up. Right now we're using these devices because they're what we have, but there is something out there that's going to change it. It just hasn't been invented yet."

For Mike the battle continues, and there is a certain level of spirituality in the practice of trying to get voices, much like the study of scripture in an attempt to get closer to God. "It strikes a cord with me. We're only scratching the surface. This information is available to us by design. It's not an accident. It's going to be the new age of man when the bridge is finally laid down and the information really flows. People are trying to find the whole grail to open it all up."

The Haunted Town Hall

I n the most notoriously haunted area of New England, in the heart of what is known as a cursed Triangle, there are bound to be a few public places known to be frequented by ghosts. There is more than a touch of the supernatural outside of the abandoned asylums and cemeteries that become home to legends and town gossip. While rumors persist about haunted restaurants and coffee shops, most are either denied by the owners and employees or used to promote the business. There are other buildings where people walk around in the light of day, rubbing elbows with the *other side* and not knowing when the lights go out that these spirits scream to be heard. In Massachusetts, where so many of our public buildings are second hand homes passed down to the town through wills, the chance of having your local real estate office or hairdresser studio be haunted increases.

Long before *Mysterious America* and the Bridgewater Triangle there was the East Bridgewater Town Hall and the stories about an old handicapped woman who still rode the elevator and walked the halls that used to be her home. The government building is now home to most of the town's offices, including the police station, but for several generations it was a private estate used by the Hobart family and their descendents. Today it remains a beautiful home from the outside, three floors with old fashion window decorations and trim suited for the wealthy of another time, but inside people are conducting business and talking about Mrs. Hobart when the clock ends and they know they can leave.

People have talked about the ghosts for decades, but the history of the house is still somewhat hidden. Aaron Hobart was a United States Representative of Massachusetts in the nineteenth century, and a man well respected by his Founding

Father companions. Either he or his son built the house, although modern records favor Aaron Hobart senior as at least the man who lived in the house after it was converted from the old Brazillai Allen Estate in 1816. His son lived there with his first wife who died in childbirth and then his second, who is believed to still be in the building, trying to deal with today's modern technology.

Why the second Mrs. Hobart's spirit is the one said to be in the house is unknown. Over time, she has been the one locals have attached to the activity in the building. She has been known to play with the lights and turn computers on and off. She is also the one responsible for one of the more unusual features of the building. In one of the offices there is a door that leads to a blocked off wall. It is accessible only from the room and has not been in use for as long as anyone can remember. The door has been known to rattle where there is no wind or extreme movement in the building, and several times people have heard knocking coming from the other side.

It is known that Mrs. Hobart was handicapped, and because she belonged to a wealthy family, she had one of the first private elevators installed in the house to help her get around. Although the original elevator has been removed and updated, she is said to still haunt it. On dozens of occasions the elevator has started by itself and traveled to different floors with no one inside. This often happens at night when there are few people around, and has been reported by the custodian of the building when no one else has had access to it. It sometimes travels to and from the basement...a feat made impossible by the fact a key is needed to get to the cellar.

The town hall was the trigger for Anne Kerrigan when she began her public access show "East Bridgewater's Most Haunted." When she began, she knew nothing of the Triangle, but she knew people had talked about the ghost of Hobart. It was the first place they investigated for the show, hosted by Mike Markowicz, and a place she feels might be home to at least one spirit. "I think there is something legitimate there. I don't have a problem saying there is a presence there. Other people are like, 'Hey, it's the town hall,' but there is something in that building."

During their investigation they received several compelling EVPs, including one that asked them to stop asking questions and another that said the ghost, presumed to be Mrs. Hobart, was happy. One even said it like the elevator because she liked to "push buttons." During the filming of the show there were several times when the pipes made an odd sound, not familiar or common to those who work in the building, and this is where some of Mike's strongest communications came from. He refers to it as 'sound remodulation,' or a spirit using the energy from one sound to talk.

The team also witnessed a light go out while they shot outside of the building. As they passed by one of the offices with the camera, the light shut off by itself. All of them were locked and no one else was in the building, so it baffled Kerrigan when it happened. "Even if it was a computer going into sleep mode, there was no one in the office. Why would the computer even be on that late?"

While faulty wiring and sensitive equipment can excuse many of the occurrences experienced by "East Bridgewater's Most Haunted" and the happenings reported by the employees, it cannot take away from the fact people who work there believe it to be haunted. While no one has ever seen the ghost, enough have felt the temperature drop too quickly or the mood in a room change or heard some noise left unexplained. The personal stories sell the haunting, and most who have a story to tell have no problem sharing their space with a ghost.

The Children
and the Angry Old Lady

I'm going to break a hard and fast rule of mine. I never write in the first person when I tell a ghost story. I keep myself out of it for two reasons. The first might be obvious. If I write the story and insert myself into it, it feels as if I am making it up, like it is somehow more fictitious. Isn't it convenient that a person who studies the paranormal has a ghost story about himself? The other is of much more importance to me. I am not the story. The people I speak to are genuine, and the stories they share are unnerving, or uplifting or frightening enough on their own without my commentary. They are very real to those who experience them, and I add nothing by talking about myself. I like for my research to stand on its own. I am not the story.

In Acushnet, that is not quite the case. There was something in the house long before I ever arrived with my tape recorder and video camera and something touched the family living there before they ever contacted me. My direct involvement with whatever haunts the house has increased the activity and made it more intense for the families that live there. The ghosts there know me and greet the investigators I work with when we get there, and unlike other ghosts I have come in contact with, the spirits want me there. They urge the residents to talk and invite us back. They want to communicate, but recent developments make me feel it is not for the purest of reasons.

My first contact with Katie, the owner of the house on Main Street, was an e-mail she sent me after hearing I was looking for ghost stories about Freetown. She was the mother of two with another on the way and studying for her nursing certification. She thought her house might be haunted, but she lived in Acushnet, a few towns over. Would I still be interested in checking it out? She and her husband, John, would love to have me over to look things over and hear her story. The discussion would be a good break from books and notes.

The stairs the children have been known to run up and down.

Two things about the house made me want to make the trip. The first was the way Katie communicated with me. She was into the paranormal, but was not overjoyed to have a ghost in her house. Until that time, there had never been any threats or anything malicious about the spirits she shared her home with, and she came off as more curious than frightened and more inquisitive than excited. The other reason was the house had been a funeral home.

The original parts of the house, which is now mainly the kitchen, was built before 1775, although no exact date can be found. It is known the property passed hands several times after 1742 before Dr. Samuel West was known to live there and before it became known by his name. The land housed a church, where West may have been a minister, and a cemetery as well, and much later it passed to an owner who added onto the house significantly. Somewhere over the next two centuries it inherited the name Kenyon and is referred to in older books as the Samuel West House and the West-Kenyon House.

In the 1920s it became a funeral home, and by that time it had expanded to two floors and more than twice its original size. Bodies were shown in what are now the master bedroom and the bedroom of the second youngest child, a boy who talks openly about the ghosts he has seen in his room. "It looked beautiful then," Katie says when she sees pictures of the former house. "It needs a lot of TLC now." The building looks strong and stable, but there are those small imperfections that make a house a home. A closer look reveals things are slightly askew. Doorways that used to be walls and stairs that are slightly off center and its railing do not line up perfectly. The more they improve the house, the more the family's personality comes through, but with each renovation, something new reveals itself.

Katie first moved into the house with her ex-boyfriend and went about the work of repairing the damage done by the old tenants. She had not been told the history of the house, including the fact it had been a funeral home decades before. The old owner had been a local police officer from Dartmouth who had not stayed long in the house, although it is uncertain whether he had experienced things in the place. Whispers say he did, but there is nothing concrete or confirmed. The closing had been a nightmare and the old owners had not shown up. The house was in serious disrepair, and things needed to be stored away before renovations could begin.

Little things began to happen that hinted something might be unusual about the house. "We would go up into the attic and there's a little door there up to the eve. There's a turn lock. We would go in there and put stuff in, close it, and next day we would go up and it would be wide open." The third floor alarmed the whole family, but as they forced the old tenants out and spent more time on the second floor, they noticed there was something living there not paying rent. "We were using the bathroom upstairs while we were working on our bathroom," explains Katie. "You'd get the weirdest feeling. Just real eerie. You'd want to leave quick."

After those initial warnings, whatever was in the house made itself known very quickly to the family, although it wasn't always obvious until they started piecing their experiences together. People take time to learn the noises of their environments, and the family was forgiving of the creaks and footsteps that seemed to come from nowhere. Doors would open and close by themselves, and at times they would hear knocks on doors inside the house where no one could be. A crock-pot fell off the counter in the kitchen and shattered. Everything was easy to explain away, but they were starting to become aware that things were happening too often.

Katie was the first to come into contact with something she could not explain away easily. "I was on the phone and could hear noises over the monitor. Like a little whispering noise, but kind of static. You would get to the door and it would stop. I would come back out and it would start again." It made no sense, but monitors often pick up radio signals. Looking back, Katie is not convinced of the reasons she gave herself. It was the first real sign something was wrong.

While sitting on the couch one night Katie heard scratching on the wall near her head. "I thought it was John sneaking up on me." She turned and the scratching stopped, but began again as if someone was running his or her nails down the cover hiding the heater ten feet away on a different wall. "I said, 'I'm out of here,' turned the TV off and went to bed."

Katie's children soon had their own experiences. "They hear their name called all the time," says Katie. "They think it's me and I'll tell them it wasn't. John hears it too, but the kids hear it all the time." One night while lying in bed, her six-year-old son Ceileachan saw an old woman come through the wall and walk across the room, disappearing through the other wall. Katie believes her son wouldn't lie, but feels he might be too young to fully understand what he saw or to not be influenced by the fact the family talks openly about the haunting. Her older daughter claims to have seen things and has a fear of the basement. "Nicole is terrified of the basement. She won't go down there."

Even the family dog, often the first indicator something might be haunting the house, had its own incident. "She was very playful, but strong. It seemed like when she was around, things happened a lot more." In addition to responding to people that could not be seen, she played a short game of fetch with someone in the bedroom. One of her toys, a cong, was stuck under the bed and she growled at it from the next room. "The cong came shooting out from underneath," claims John. "It rolled out. She grabbed it and ran out. Before that Katie was telling me stories and I was like, 'Okay, sure.' I never believed her."

While there were signs of a ghost in the house, it wasn't until the house changed residents that the activity really began. Katie's mother, who had been living on the third floor, moved out and Kurt and his fiancé Jen moved into the second floor. The original residents in the house when they had moved in four years earlier had been destructive and annoying, but Kurt and Jen were their polar opposites. Kurt helped to repair the house and brought his gigantic cockatoo to change the atmosphere.

"Things really changed when my mother left," says Katie. "It wasn't easy when she was here, but when she left, whatever was here kind of left. It moved upstairs. Whoever is here is taking an interest in us."

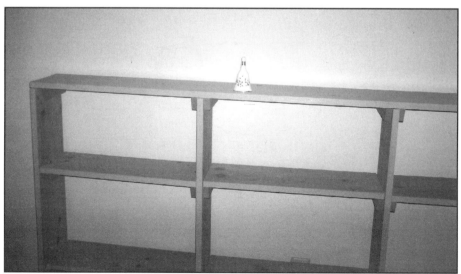

One of the active rooms in the house and the bell the spirits ring.

Both families began to hear footsteps running up and down the stairs on a regular basis, sometimes heavy and deliberate, other times the sound of a child or children running from one of the upstairs rooms down the hall, down the stairs and across the landing where Kurt and Jen's apartment is. Sometimes there would be knocking on walls and doors, and those doors would later open by themselves. Kurt once heard his front door knock loud and clear while he was watching television. He got up to get the door, expecting it to be Katie or John. "He opened the door and nobody was there," remembers Katie.

It is hard to admit the paranormal might be sharing the house with you, and the families continued to make excuses for the things that were happening. Kurt has children of his own who come and stay with them, and between all the children and friends and relatives, some running is expected. Katie started to face an odd truth. "This would happen when no one was around. The kids would be gone, and you'd hear banging and running. Sometimes it was like they were running a race or something. You can't ignore that and I know I'm not crazy, especially because Jen and Kurt hear it too. He heard them talking in the attic."

The families were beginning to get uncomfortable in the house. At times there was a certain charm to having a ghost, but it was becoming a little overwhelming. "Nicole hates living here and won't be alone," says Katie. "John gets the creeps going into the attic." Both Ceileachan and John share a fear of moving things up into storage and kid each other about who has to do it. "Ceileachan has said he doesn't want the ghosts to get him."

Then there is the strange smell. "Like sewer," says Kurt who has smelled the garbage odor in the house more than once. The smell follows people in the house around, sometimes effecting only one person in a room while the other cannot smell anything. It can happen at anytime and in any room of the house. John first smelled it in the basement. "I went down into the basement to do the laundry and I got that smell." It does not last long, and leaves as suddenly as it arrives. He has worked with trash and waste before and says the smell is something different, not the sweet but off-putting smell of some waste. Kurt is more concerned about how it leaves the house. "As quickly as it comes up, it goes away."

If there are ghosts in they house, they seem to be feeding off the emotion there, flaring up at times of high intensity and when things are going very well or when there is a high level of stress. The giggles and running increase when there are many children in the house and then continues after they leave, as if their energy is left and then recycled by the spirits. John is unsure why, but he sees the pattern. "It's always when we're doing something."

One Thanksgiving Nicole was upstairs in Kurt and Jen's apartment when she heard her door wiggling, like some one was trying to get in. A voice called her name, and was heard by two other girls in the room. No one was there and the three did not hear anyone move away or go down the stairs.

One day John was making a decision about a major job change that would dramatically alter the family's lifestyle. He had dropped off his resume and went home to try and relax. He was in the shower, "stressed big time," and thinking about what to do, when a ball of light, about the size of a baseball, passed before his eyes and through the shower curtain into the bathroom. He quickly pulled it back to follow the light, but it was gone. The bathroom has no windows and the door was tightly closed. "It just flew by and then into nothing. The only light in here was from the candle, and the curtains are heavy. There is no way any light gets in."

"Christmas Eve we all heard running up and down the front hallway staircase. Kurt heard it between 3:30 to 6 (p.m.) when my children were not home. I heard it when I went to bed at 12:15 and my children were asleep." The activity on Christmas encouraged Katie to try and make contact. Earlier she had read something about placing a bell for the spirit to try and talk through. Since then all members of the family have heard the bell ring when no one is up in the attic and there is no wind.

She decided to get more hands on. "I don't know if I am not supposed to engage them or not, but one morning I had to go into the attic to look for something. On my way out of the attic to the stairway I said, 'OK, Have a good day', then pulled the string for the light. Halfway down the staircase I heard the unmistakable click of the pull chain being clicked back on. I just said, 'OK. See you later.' I didn't know what else to say."

The activity only increased as two new emotional elements entered into the equation. Jen and Kurt were to be married and Katie learned she was pregnant with her third child. Things started happening more frequently and the nature of the hauntings became more intense. Katie began seeing a dark shadow out of the corner of her eye. The couple's sleep began to be disturbed. "I get my name called all the time," says John. "It will wake me up in the middle of the night. I'll think it's Katie, and she'll be laying right next to me, asleep." Another time he woke up from a vivid dream to see the bedroom closet open on its own. The door is heavy and the floor in front of it slightly warped, making it hard to open and close. "As soon as it started to open and I saw it, the door stopped." Both have felt a pressure on the bed at night, as if someone is coming to lie down next to them.

The real activity was happening on the second floor, and however much they tried to ignore it, Kurt and Jen knew something was just outside their door. The doorbell was going off at odd times during the night or there was a pounding on the door or the wall inside their room. "I was in the bathroom and I heard the doorbell ring," says Kurt. He went to the door and no one was there. Another time the door opened by itself. "I knew the door was closed. I know I locked it. You have to. Whatever it is, just wanted in." After going through all the logical arguments and coming to a dead end, he has now embraced what might be there. He believes small children are trapped in the house for reasons he cannot explain. "I know their knocking on that door. It's two in the morning and everyone's asleep."

He also knows they are there because he hears them. "The conversations sound like their right outside the door. We can hear them talking right out there in the hallway. I mean, you can hear them talking clearly. I can hear the voices, I just can't hear what they're saying. It sounds like gibberish." Most of the time there is just a child's laugh.

The woman and the children she speaks to are the primary ghosts in the house, and she may be easier to identify than the other elements living there. While they are unsure if there were any children who lived in the house, they do know something about a former owner. She was an older woman named Ms. Senigal, who was known to keep an immaculate house and to like things in order. "An old lady lived here for a while," explains Kurt. "She was a nanny and traveling companion." According to records, she suffered an accident in the house and died a short time later. This may be the old woman Ceileachan saw in his room, and it might explain something else that was happening in the house.

Several members of the household have heard her voice. "It sounds soft," says John. "Like when your mother is trying to wake you up."

The voice is never threatening, but one night Kurt was witness to how stern it could be. "It woke me up at 2 o'clock in the morning. I thought it was Katie. She was yelling at someone. She was saying, 'The room is a mess. You need to pick things up.'" Kurt believes the woman was disciplining children in the house, almost as if he was hearing a recording of a day in the life of her family. She was not yelling, but was stern in telling the children the room was too messy and they needed to clean their mess. Despite the normality of what she was saying, the incident remains one of the most vivid and disturbing for him.

When I first met the family it was just before Katie's test and I was surprised at the warmth of the house. I arrived with Matt Moniz, scientist, paranormal expert and researcher, and science advisor for the paranormal talk radio show "Spooky Southcoast." We walked through the room with nothing more than our cameras and tape recorders, listening to the couple tell us about what they had experienced there and tracing the ghosts' activities. Everything felt normal. It was a lived-in family house, far from anything you would read about in a ghost book or a tale of the dead.

And then we went upstairs to the third floor.

It was as if our creaks on the stairs alerted them we were there. Before he stepped onto the landing Matt asked if I had heard that. "Right as we were going up I heard a voice. It was loud enough that I heard it with no equipment. It said 'hello.'" The makeshift office had a few books and bit of old furniture, including a bookcase with the bell on it.

When we went into the old bedroom Matt and I immediately stared at each other. I often feel I was not blessed with any sensitivity, and Matt is firmly planted in the world of science. We both sensed there was something wrong with the room. I felt sick and had to leave, and Matt concentrated himself at trying to get some pictures and EVPs from it.

The room was small but sparse, with an old unplugged miniature refrigerator and a mattress standing on its side. The

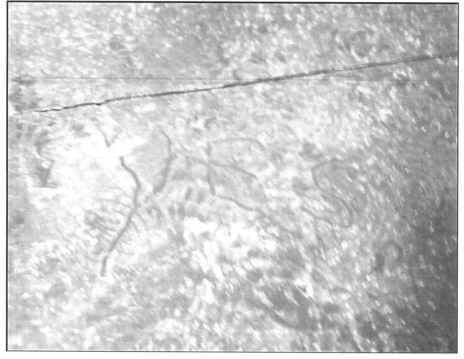

**A picture taken of the ghostly message written in baby powder.
The "yes" can clearly be seen.**

oppressive heat that almost suffocated us as we reached the top floor was now concentrated there, making it harder to breath and think. My tape recorder, video camera and flashlight, all with brand new batteries, went dead and I left to escape the heat and switch equipment.

When I arrived back upstairs we decided to do a quick EVP session in Matt's unique way. Unlike many investigators who ask very direct questions or antagonize spirits to get a response, Matt does not ask questions about why they are in the house or if their spirit is trapped. Instead he asks them everyday questions you might ask a living person you meet for the first time. "I ask them their favorite food or what kind of music they like. They're simple questions I can either verify later or that might make sense later on in the investigation." Matt also feels the questions put the spirit at ease and are less rude or intrusive than some of the more standard questions. An intelligent spirit on the other side might be more willing to talk to someone it can respect.

After a while we decided to close down for the night. We had intended the initial investigation to be nothing more than a walkthrough of the house and a handshake with the owners and the couple on the second floor. We decided a second investigation, planned and with more equipment, was necessary and needed to be done as soon as possible. Matt was most intrigued by the old bedroom. "There was something in that room. I didn't get any evidence yet, but it's there."

I was going through the evidence with a class of high school kids. As part of the school week, they engaged in one fun activity outside of their normal routine, and I ran an elective on paranormal investigating. We sat down with some of the audio from the night and I showed them how to search for odd noises and voices on the tapes. Several shouted out to stop after I asked the question, "Do you know our names?" Everyone in the room, fifteen teenagers in all, all heard a low male voice coming through the speakers.

"Matthew," it said in its singsong voice.

There were several other voices recorded, including a reference to the name Dillon, a name that would come up in future communications.

We were anxious to get back and try and record more evidence. We recruited Matt's associate Lucky, a professional photographer, and Mike Markowicz, a well-respected EVP specialist from East Bridgewater. We again toured the house, spending more time in Kurt and Jen's apartment and snapping pictures while Mike set up his elaborate recording system through the second and third floor. As we finished setting up and arrived back downstairs and prepared to walk outside, the lights in the front hallway dimmed, flashed three times and then stayed on. The evening was casual, as we just left the tapes rolling and went outside with the family to go over some of the evidence we had gotten the first time there.

What Mike recorded changed our ideas on ghosts. "There was just constant chatter," Mike found. "You can't understand all of it, but the voices are all there." There seemed to have been several different spirits in the house, which does not mean the spirits are always there. Sometimes spirits are drawn to investigators, and the transient spirit nature of a funeral home might invite people who had helped with the dead's transition to stay.

Mike recorded examples of laughing, singing and talking, but the majority of the EVPs were in the form of whispers. This could be due to several things, including power and frequency issues. The spirits are too weak to come out louder. There might be another reason. The house might be a way station for spirits because of the previous activity, but also because of its use as a funeral home for several decades.

In addition to the old woman who is thought to haunt the house, there were at least two other males, a second woman and several children. Most of the voices made no sense, like walking into a room and hearing only part of a story. He recorded a voice saying, "dreadful," and another saying, "that's neat," right before fireworks go off in the background. Different voices say, "they're laying down," and "get packing," while another says "smoke crack and you'll never go back."

Others are more disturbing. A female is heard saying, "If you love me don't hit me again," and "I love you," which is sung in a low volume. There are several references to killing, both from a male and a female voice. There are names said, none of which hold any meaning to the history of the house, except Mike's name is whispered and someone asks for Kate.

There were several examples of the spirits seeming to know we were there. They refer to us and several times make reference to wanting to talk or telling other spirits to not talk to us or be heard. They mention several names, but it is unclear if they are talking to each other or people that are not there. There are conversations that point to a debate on what we are doing and whether it is okay to go along with us.

> **First Male:** "Hi, fellas."
> **Second Male:** "It was beautiful, absolutely beautiful."
> **Third Male:** *"Let's not give in. Let's clear the air."*
> **Second Male:** "Is there anyone in here?"
> **Third Male:** *"Who cares?"*
> **Second Male:** "I'll say."

Another conversation seems to be directed to us. A male voice is heard as a car drives by and then a female responds, "Interesting comment. I don't want them in my house." The story does say the older woman didn't respond well the children in the house, and there are other references made to the children throughout the tape, but it is unclear if she is referring to the children or us.

There are several ghosts present in the house, and they are operating on different levels. There is not as much known about the paranormal as some may present. It is unknown whether these ghosts are on different levels of consciousness or in different dimensions. They might be diverse energy sources, some taking the form of residual hauntings while others are the fully thinking kind. Even on that level, there are different intelligences or stairs of understanding. The children make themselves known, while some of the adults try to force them to stop talking. Some can see us, while some are walking in the dark. Something bigger might be playing with everyone.

We left with proof of something, but we weren't sure of what it all meant. A few weeks later we returned to share what we had found and to try and get some visual evidence. We brought along Thomas D'Agostino and his wife Arlene. As Mike shared his evidence with the family, everyone else set up the equipment, but the ghosts were already starting to talk.

Almost immediately, Tom's digital tape picked up voices. They recognized us and had learned something about us. "What we experienced was EVPs that were mimicking us. It was as if the energy was intelligent and aware of who each of us was." On tape the voices would echo what we were saying, and then they began to say our words before we would. "I said, 'Hello again,' four times while entering the office room. The fourth time something said hello again before I did." Both Matt and Tom heard the repeating on several of their recordings.

Matt sees the communication as a bit devious. "They are playing with us. Tom's questions are answered on my recorder and my questions are answered on his."

Tom also got an interesting EVP of someone looking for a bit of normality on the other side. Arlene came up the stairs and asked what was wrong with the house. A humble voice, heard only on tape, said, "Nothing."

Mike, who heard small children giggling on his recordings on that third night, is intrigued by the house, and is at a lose to explain all that might be going on. "The house is owned by genuinely warm people and the feel of the house reflects the same. I never felt creeped out upon entering that place and I believe the spirits that are visiting or living there as it may are decent as well. It's just a spiritually active house, that's all."

The evidence he is gathering there is beyond what he has heard before. "The EVPs seem almost a constant as men woman and children appear to be living their lives along with the current owners. When you look at the evidence as a whole you can get an idea of just how the house is behaving. It's a house worth studying because it represents just what the next life is all about, living. And the EVP I recorded of the man saying, 'Come on children, it's time to go,' shows us that an apparent man is in charge of caring for at least two children and they are going somewhere. This may have happened in the past but it is happening for someone. People are still caring for people even when they pass on."

After the last investigation, a curious thing happened. Kurt's bird was moved inside and that, along with our having gone in, sparked something more. The running of the children intensified and began to be heard more often. They were now running right outside his door and up the stairs. Once he heard it as his bird watched invisible children run by the cage and into the darkness, following the noise with his head.

Kurt then talked to the ghosts, trying to make contact, and got nothing in return. He had recently put out talcum powder, as we had requested, to try and get some physical evidence of a presence. He asked why they did not want to talk to him and asked if they were scared of him. The next day, when he went to the attic, the word, "Yes," was messily written in the powder. No one in the family had been up there. There was also a large footprint. The size was too big for anyone in the house, and was barefoot.

He then asked the children into the apartment, inviting them to come in and play with the bird. This may have been a mistake on his part. The darker elements of the paranormal, such as demons, hide in the shadows after a human ghost has made initial contact. They go along for the ride and play as if they are the original ghost, all the time waiting for an invitation to take the situation to a scarier level. Kurt might have invited something evil in.

I told him it was probably a bad idea until we had done more work in the house, and he agreed. He told them they were no longer allowed in, and things began to get extreme. The slamming doors increased, happening several times a night instead of once in a while, and the television began to turn on and off by itself. Something did not like being asked to leave.

One night after the invite, Jen was woken up by weight on the bed and a hand on her shoulder. She opened her eyes, and heard footsteps, like a child, running out of the room. She also heard faint giggling.

Katie and her family, even with the new baby, have not seen an increase in activity, but that is nothing new. "They leave us alone now." She hears the things Kurt and Jen talk about, but it is not in her part of the house, almost like it is not happening to her. There is a hesitation when she thinks about turning on her baby monitor when the baby sleeps.

A good ghost story, most times, has some kind of conclusion. There is a resolution to the problem. We find the source of the haunting or the ghost realizes there is something better and moves on. A vital clue makes itself known, usually though our outside research, and we make the connection. The Samuel West does not have the resolution. It remains, as Mike said, a place we need to investigate because of the unique haunting there. The case is ongoing, and evolving every time we visit or discuss it. I would like to say the hauntings remain harmless and something more intriguing than frightening, but Kurt's calls come later in the night and there is an increasing urgency to his voice.

Some stories just go on and on...

And That's Only the Beginning

There is a famous ghost at the Wareham Public Library. She is said to maybe have been a librarian, and wanted peace and quiet near her collection. Above all, she hated rock music and thought it disturbed her readers, especially when people would drive by the library with their radios turned up. She was known in life to run out and chase cars that played their music too loud as they passed and encourage them to listen to classical music instead. She is still discouraging the corruption of youth and holding up Mozart as the key to happiness. In her death she is said to change the radio station of cars that pass by. If the volume is too loud, she will turn it to a local classical station.

No name is ever given for the librarian, and in fact, she never really existed. The uncommon occurrence in Wareham has nothing to do with a ghost. It just so happens that right on that spot is a weird split in the town's radio reception. Near that spot is a convergence of two different radio stations. One is a rock station and the other a classical, and a radio with weak reception will switch between the two as it drives down the street.

Welcome to the Triangle. Stories like that exist side by side with horrific tales of dark men who take your very breath away. Hauntings are developed over generations, but some have their basis in the personal experiences of everyday people living today. The tales from the Triangle are bipolar and sometimes elusive; they surface just long enough for the questions to come up. These have only been a few of them, and the stories continue to come in.

There is the haunted library in Fairhaven people have talked about for years and the second oldest house in Bridgewater with an active haunting. More Pukwudgie stories come in all the time, and I didn't even touch upon the murder in a Brockton hotel witnessed by two employees years after. Did I mention the Bridgewater State Hospital is one of the oldest and most controversial mental health hospitals in the country? The Triangle draws these stories in and invites tragedy and the paranormal with the same hand. A complete book of the happenings there would be more like an ongoing conversation than the kind of story you could sit with and close the book after it is done. There is no "done."

The Bridgewater Triangle is a living, breathing thing, and it does not rest while its stories are told. Much like the ocean, if you are not careful, it will sneak up on you. The lines defined by Loren Coleman twenty-five years ago continue to expand, and the whole lore the land will never be complete. Sometimes it is enough just to brace yourself and get caught up in the waves.

Bibliography

"Aaron Hobart." Wikipedia. Retrieved November 2, 2007; http://en.wikipedia.org/wiki/Aaron_Hobart.

"Abandoned Photography and Urban Exploration: Making The Best Out Of Haunted Locations Throughout New England." Retrieved October 25, 2007; www.freewebs.com/eidolicvisitors/location.htm.

Ariel Sabar. "'Ghost Writer' Tells Tales from the Crypt." *The Providence Journal*. October 31, 1998.

Balzano, Christopher. *Dark Woods: Cults, Crime and the Paranormal in the Freetown State Forest*. Atglen, Pennsylvania: Schiffer Publishing Ltd., 2008.

"Beware the Bridgewater Triangle." *The Comment*. Retrieved September 24, 2007; http://www.bsccomment.com/media/paper662/news/2003/10/30/CampusNews/Beware.Of.The.Triangle-544610.shtml

Brunvard, Jan Harold. *The Encyclopedia of Urban Legends*. Santa Barbara, California: ABC-CLIO, Inc., 2001.

Cadieux, Aaron. "Inside the Bridgewater Triangle." Big Operations Productions, 2003. (Film.)

Citro, Joseph. *Strange Passing: True Tales of New England Hauntings and Horrors*. New York, New York: Houghton Mifflin Company, 1996.

Curious New England: The Unconventional Traveler's Guide to Eccentric Destinations. Lebanon, New Hampshire: University Press of New England, 2003.

D'Agostino, Thomas. *Haunted Massachusetts.* Atglen, Pennsylvania: Schiffer Publishing Ltd, 2007.

Haunted Rhode Island. Atglen, Pennsylvania: Schiffer Publishing Ltd, 2006.

"Fire at old Foxborough State Hospital." WHDH-TV Online. Retrieved October 14, 2007; http://www3.whdh.com/news/articles/local/BO22769.

Fritz, Jean. *The Good Giants and the Bad Pukwudgies.* New York, New York: G. P. Putnam's Sons, 1983.

"Fort Adams Unofficial Site." Retrieved November 10, 2007. http://www.geocities.com/~jmgould/fortadams.html.

Gerry Tuoti. "Creepy Cemetery Tales." *The Taunton Gazette.* October 31, 2005.

"Ghosts of Wheaton." *The Sun Chronicle Online.* Retrieved October 13, 2007. http://www.sunchronicle.com/articles/2006/11/01/features/feature28.txt.

Greer, John Michael. *The New Encyclopedia of the Occult.* St. Paul, Minnesota: Llewellyn Publications, 2003.

Howland, Franklin. *A History of the Town of Acushnet.* New Bedford, Massachusetts: Franklin Howland, 1907.

Lodi, Edward. *Ghosts from King Philip's War.* Middleborough, Massachusetts: Rock Village Publishing, 2006.

The Haunted Violin. Middleborough, Massachusetts: Rock Village Publishing, 2005.

"The Mad Trucker of Copicutt Road." *New England Legends*. Retrieved August 24, 2006. www.freewebs.com/newenglandlegends/madtruckfreetown.htm.

Marcus, Jon. *Unknown New England: Landmarks, Museums, and Historical Sites You Never Knew Existed*. Bloomington, Indiana: 1st Books, 2003.

"Massachusetts Ghost Hauntings." *Ghosts of America*. Retrieved May 5, 2007. www.ghostsofamerica.com/states/ma.html

"NEA Massachusetts." *New England Anomalies*. Retrieved August 17, 2007. www.newenglandanomaly.com/massachusetts/massachusetts.htm.

Reynard, Elizabeth. *The Narrow Land: Folk Chronicles of Old Cape Cod*. Chatham, Massachusetts: The Chatham Historical Society, Inc., 1978.

Robinson, Charles Turek. *The New England Ghost Files an Authentic Compendium of Frightening Phantoms*. North Attleboro, Massachusetts: Covered Bridge Press, 1994.
True New England Mysteries, Ghosts, Crimes, and Oddities. North Attleboro, Massachusetts: Covered Bridge Press, 1994.

Scammel, Henry. *Mortal Remains: Bizarre Serial Killings Stun a Small New England Town*. New York, New York: HaperPaperbacks, 1991.

Sharp, Eleyne Austen. *Haunted Newport*. Newport, Rhode Island: Austen Sharp, 1999.

Smith, Carlton. *Killing Season: The Unsolved Case of New England's Deadliest Serial Killer*. New York, New York: Onyx Books, 1994.

Spitler, Scott. "History Up in Flames." *The Taunton Gazette*. March 26, 2006.

"USGenWeb Brockton, 1905 Boiler Explosion." US GenWeb Brockton. Retrieved September 21, 2006. www.rootsweb. com/~macbrock/boiler.html.

"Visiting a Graveyard at Foxboro State Hospital." *Squaring the Boston Globe*. Retrieved October 14, 2007. http:// squaringtheglobe.blogspot.com/2004/07/visiting-graveyard-at-foxboro-state.html.

"Website tells rumored tales of possible haunted buildings on campus." *The Comment*. Retrieved November 4, 2007. http:// media.www.bsccomment.com/media/storage/paper662/ news/2007/10/25/CampusNews/Website.Tells.Rumored. Tales.Of.Possible.Haunted.Buildings.On.Campus-3060083. shtml.

Index

Achushnet, 201-215
Alves, Alan, 15, 30, 125
Assawompset Pond, 48-49, 49
Attleboro, 81, 177, 185

Barrett, Jackie, 136
Bridgewater, 14, 15, 20, 22, 23, 71, 122, 142, 217, 218
Bridgewater State College, 6, 142
Bridgewater State Hospital, 20, 218
Broadway Street Cemetery, 84
Brockton, 8, 90-93, 218

Clark and Horr Cemetery, 85
Coleman, Loren, 7-11, 14, 20, 21, 26, 108, 218

D'Agostino, Thomas, 167, 214

East Bridgewater, 7, 198, 212
East Bridgewater's Most Haunted, 199-200
Easton, 10, 151, 158-159
Ellis Bolles Cemetery, 85-86

Fairhaven, 26, 81, 141, 166, 183, 217
Fairhaven High School, 141

Fall River, 27, 54, 82-83, 128, 137, 180
Fort Adams, 168-171, 164, 165, 166, 169
Foxboro, 71-77, 72, 75
Freetown, 8, 15, 18, 19, 23, 24, 26-38, 36, 39, 40, 90, 118, 128, 166, 187, 201,

Hornbine School, 108, 110

King Philip, 26, 41, 42, 43, 46, 47, 48, 158-159
King Philip's War, 15, 21, 24, 39, 42, 46, 128

Lakeville, 48, 85
Lizzie Borden, 24, 54, 82, 127-137
Lizzie Borden Bed and Breakfast, 127-137, 106, 107, 127, 131
Lodi, Edward, 46, 47

Marion, 141
Markowicz, Mike, 192-197, 199, 212, 214, 216
Massasoit, 39, 41
Mattapoisett, 86
Middleboro, 46, 96
Mount Hope Cemetery, 83-84

New Bedford, 44, 86, 166, 176, 180, 183-184

Newport, Rhode Island, 13, 166-171

North Attleboro, 83-84

Norton, 8, 10, 146-149

Old Village Cemetery, 95, 98-105 102, 103

Onset, 172-174

Palmer River Burial Grounds, 94, 95-98, 78, 79, 94

Pukwudgies, 31-34, 32, 37, 49

Rehoboth, 8, 10, 13, 33, 42, 43, 44, 94-105, 108-126

Riverside Cemetery, 81

Robinson, Charles, 16, 43, 95, 100, 104, 108-116, 118, 126

Rochester, 86, 176

Seekonk, 117, 126

Spooky Southcoast, 44, 113, 209

St. Stephen's Cemetery, 81-82

Stonehill College, 150-163, 138, 139, 150, 155, 160

Tabor Academy, 141

Taunton, 8, 9, 23, 52-59, 60-70, 71, 77, 84-85, 168

Taunton State Hospital, 50, 51, 52 52-59, 70, 168

Wampanoag, 33, 38, 39, 45, 47, 48

Wheaton College, 143, 146-149

Wareham, 172-174, 175, 217